RETAIL
DEVELOPMENT

By the same author

Retail Site Assessment

published by Business Books Limited

RETAIL
DEVELOPMENT

ROGER COX

BUSINESS BOOKS LIMITED   LONDON

First published 1972

© ROGER KENNETH COX

0 220 99249 5

*This book has been set in 10 on 11pt. Imprint
and printed by C. Tinling & Co. Ltd., London and Prescot
for the publishers Business Books Limited
(registered office: 180 Fleet Street, London, E.C.4)
publishing office: Mercury House, Waterloo Road, London, S.E.1*

MADE AND PRINTED IN GREAT BRITAIN

CONTENTS

LIST OF TABLES

LIST OF FIGURES AND PLATES

viii

ACKNOWLEDGEMENTS

The author wishes to acknowledge with thanks all the sources mentioned below.

Mothercare Ltd. for personal help and permission to reproduce illustrations and J. Sainsbury Ltd, the John Lewis Partnership, Fine Fare Ltd and F. W. Woolworth Ltd for permission to reproduce illustrations. In addition, the author wishes to thank Montagu Evans & Son and particularly Mr L. V. Trott of John Trott & Son for kind permission to reproduce Appendix I, and Mr Ralph G. Towsey A.C.I.S. of the National Cash Register Company Limited for personal help, guidance and permission to use quotations.

The author also wishes to thank all other individuals and organisations not mentioned above for their help in writing this book.

JAMES

I

STRATEGY AND TECHNIQUES

There is one well tried and relatively painless method of producing an apparent improvement in company results and that is to alter the bases of the company's accounting procedures. Another, but more arduous, method is to institute and progress formal planning systems for stimulating long term growth.

It is quite clear today that the need to plan has been fully established in most industries and in the public sector as a whole. The retail industry is no exception; perhaps the need here is intensified by the handful of special problems which the industry presents. Certainly retailers themselves sometimes like to believe that these peculiarities require a special expertise in their handling: this is usually described as 'practical experience' and lends an air of mystique to the art of shopkeeping. Management consultants have come across similar reactions in other industries, many of which have been long established and are today conservative in outlook. This is not to gainsay that there has been a 'retail revolution'. Many British multiples have successfully met the greatly changed market conditions since the last war and some of the methods they have used are described in this book. What has been lacking—and this is true of many firms—is the coordination of planning, using the appropriate techniques from the battery of accepted methods. Some of these methods are substitutable, most of them are useful and they can be marshalled to assist in the corporate planning process which is outlined in the next section.

CORPORATE PLANNING

Corporate planning has been described as the total planning of a company's entire resources for the achievement of both short and long term objectives. It is, in other words, a systematic approach to managing the whole of a firm's activities on a planned time scale into the future so that the company can anticipate and profit from change. Some writers have even seen it as a formalisation of individual management processes which are going on in most companies anyway. In fact, it provides a framework within which coordinated planning to a specific end can proceed subject to a logical phasing as given below. There are two main aspects of corporate planning. First, the company has to plan its strategy, that is decide in what direction the company should be developing. Strategic planning is concerned with the objectives and basic purpose of the company and how its resources can be mobilised to achieve these objectives. Second, the company must decide its tactics: tactical planning embraces the methods by which the strategy plans can be implemented.

PURPOSES AND PROBLEMS

The purpose of a business unit is the attainment of its long term objectives, both economic and social. The purpose of a company is therefore immutable, while the means towards achieving the purpose may change as the firm develops. An economic objective is a measurement of the efficiency of the resource-conversion process and as such can be quantified. Three factors make up the objective: the desired attribute (e.g. earnings per share), the scale of performance (e.g. average rate of return on equity) and the goal—the particular value on the scale which the firm seeks to attain (e.g. optimisation). The firm should set its objectives within the framework of an acceptable time scale which, in the case of public joint stock companies, is normally infinite.[1]

One of the basic problems facing policy makers is, of course, how to frame meaningful objectives in a long term situation. The difficulty centres on forecasting major changes in the external environment which will necessitate altering company goals. The greater the time scale or the planning period involved the greater the risk of external changes. As a result, cast iron plans committing a company to certain profit levels or investment decisions are rarely, in most industries, made for more than five years ahead. Business planning must therefore be flexible and based on a continuous cycle which involves the monitoring of actual performance against estimates and the updating of future budgets on the basis of this screening of performance.

Before any firm objectives can be set, indeed before any reasoned planning can take place, a company must take stock of its current position and then decide, on the basis of this assessment, how it wishes to develop and what its objectives are to be. Once a firm has decided on its strategy it is then able to formulate an organisation structure for carrying out the strategy and a series of operational (or tactical) plans can be set for each part of the organisation. We then have the basis of a corporate plan and a corporate identity.

THE STRATEGIC PLAN

The strategic plan outlines the objectives towards which the company plans to move and the time scale for achievement.

I ASSESSMENT OF THE CURRENT POSITION

In order to gain an insight into the real strengths and weaknesses of a company it is necessary to probe as deeply as possible and to ask a number of questions, some of which may be difficult to answer:

What business are we really in?
What are we good at?
How well are we doing? Can we extrapolate the trend confidently?
If so, is the progress good enough? Is it better than competitive firms?
And so on.

By examining the following four aspects of company operation and by getting answers to the appropriate questions, a debit–credit list for further study and action can be compiled. The reader is advised to consult J. W. Humble's *Improving Business Results*, Appendix II, for a fairly exhaustive checklist on strengths and weaknesses.

Return on capital assets Management performance in manipulating the capital resources at its disposal over the past five to ten years should be investigated with particular regard to the trend of earnings per share (which now appears to be the key measurement). Obviously, if the trends have been static or downward, the original stock of assets held by the company have either not been competently managed, or the company has not invested or divested to take cognisance of changes in the external environment. It is additionally useful to compare the firm's performance with its own industry's and with industry as a whole.

Markets Many retail firms are not aware precisely of their shares of particular markets. It is difficult in retailing to assess market shares because of the fragmentation of a multiple retailer's total market into

3

catchment area sub-markets, and also because of the wide range of different commodities that many retail firms now sell. The first approach to this problem for a retailer with national coverage is to take the firm's sales as a percentage of total retail sales and then to break this percentage down into commodity shares of market. Trends in each commodity market should be studied with a view to exploiting the opportunities thrown up and to rationalising the product range sold where there is evidence of poor contribution. Further research on local (catchment) market shares is also required by each retailer. Although notoriously difficult to secure, competitors' market shares are useful if not vital for comparison purposes. Customers make up markets and a firm, particularly in retailing, should know who they are and what influences their decisions to buy or not (e.g. price, quality or 'image').

Resource allocation   The resources of a retail firm, as in other industries, include not only capital assets in the physical sense such as freehold properties, stock, fixtures, transport fleets and so on, but monetary resources (e.g. cash in hand and at bank) and human resources such as management and worker skills. The investigation should decide what quantity of each resource is allocated to each activity in the firm to find out what the return is relative to employing these resources in the activity: the net profitability of each division or service is the result. From this it will be seen how well the company is utilising its total resources and what degree of productivity is occurring in each of its component parts. Some guide to assessment may be got from organisations such as the Centre for Interfirm Comparison and Dun and Bradstreet.

Organisation structure   This means the managerial posts in an organisation and their relationships. The investigation will show whether the company is properly organised to carry out its present commitments efficiently and whether the current objectives are spelt out in unit and individual terms from the board of directors downwards. Its present management development and succession plans and worker performance and attitudes will also come under review. (See the following chapter.)

Strengths and weaknesses   By concentrating on the four basic areas outlined above a company should be able to answer all the questions posed by itself and produce a checklist of strengths and weaknesses for further action. One of the initial results of such an investigation is that areas where immediate increases in profitability are possible are shown up, particularly under the heading of resource allocation.

The evolution of a strategy requires creative thinking, the use of simulation techniques (probably using EDP) and the financial evaluation of competing alternatives (using DCF and value analysis). After arriving at the 'best solution' or optimisation of resources it is then necessary to quantify the changes which must be made in each area of operations to match the strategy and produce a programme for each: X new shops, Y more capital, Z more management and labour and so on.[2]

2 SETTING THE OBJECTIVES

If the firm was not very clear about where it was going before, its motivations should be much less opaque after such an investigation. The prime objective for any commercial organisation is to return a satisfactory profit, and this is normally expressed as a desire to achieve a continuous growth on shareholders' equity, both in the short term and in the long. This objective can be attained by raising the firm's pre-tax return on capital employed both in the short and long term and a profit target can be set, supported by a profit forecast which must take into account the firm's strengths and weaknesses and the foreseeable changes in the form of opportunities and risks which may occur in the external environment. The environment must present actually or potentially a situation where these expectations can be met. One method of finding out is by the use of marketing research (as explained elsewhere in this book) which will take into account the economic, sociological and political factors at work outside the firm. A retail company will wish to be represented in these market sectors which not only offer greater 'customer input' but which also produce higher sales levels. Any forecasts must recognise the effect of competition in these markets.

The personalities of management must also be taken into account when assessing alternative courses of action: a chief executive may wish his firm to achieve as a prime *objective* a reputation for good quality and fair dealing in the public eye or, again, wish his firm to become the 'largest' supermarket company in Great Britain. These aspirations (subjective or not) should be recognised in any discussion on corporate planning and appropriate values put on them. So, of course, should the ethical and social aspects of company purpose; as previously stated, a secondary set of objectives in business should be to achieve certain non-economic goals such as security of tenure in employment for the company's staff. These latter goals should not for any length of time, however, override the basic economic objective of the firm.

Finally, company objectives should be framed in specific terms (*not* 'we wish to increase our market share substantially' but 'we wish to increase our market share from 3 per cent to 7 per cent over three years'); objectives should be clearly identifiable but interrelated, while not running counter to each other. They must obviously also be quantified.[2] Company objectives should also be realistic and constrained to

5

B

allow of achievement. Robert Heller in one of his caustic *Observer* pieces time, unattainable. Robert Heller in one of his caustic *Observer* pieces has pointed out the lack of realism among many boards when targets are set; this he puts down to financial ignorance or even financial guile.[3] There is surely no point in setting objectives (or even in planning as a whole) if the company does not do its damnedest to see that the goals are reached. As a case in point, one of the most potent factors in this unrealism is the dropping of budgetary controls which compare actual with past performance and substituting budgets comparing actual with *predicted* performance, thus using the forecasts both as targets and means of control.

3 PREPARING THE STRATEGIC PLAN

This section outlines the framework of the plan and its components under six headings; they are not listed in order of priority. A case study later in this chapter gives examples of objectives themselves.

Broad statement of aims This statement will outline what business the firm is in (or wishes to be in) and what general categories of product the firm retails, e.g. groceries, provisions, fresh meat, produce and selected non-foods. The firm may also state what 'image' it wishes to project to the public and its employees and suppliers.

Sales and profit requirements Details of the annual sales and profit goals for the business as a whole and for each trading activity for the year ahead, along with forecasts for the period of the plan, say 5 years, should be formulated.

Market opportunities A detailed list of geographical markets (i.e. towns and shopping centres) and existing product categories where it is felt that opportunities for profitable expansion exist should be prepared. Further market opportunities may be in other product fields, e.g. ranges of adult and children's clothing to be merchandised alongside food. The required shares for both product and geographical markets should also be estimated and built in as objectives.

Investment and divestment plans This will pinpoint those businesses which could be taken over should the opportunity arise, with their consequent effect on total profitability matched against the probable investment involved. This may involve integration backwards into production as well as horizontal integration. Divestment plans may include a list of shop disposals which may come about due to their unprofitability or because of general rationalisation of the chain. Further diversification into franchising, concession sites or into marketing/advertising/transport or other service facilities will also come under this heading.

Resource allocation and return on investment The manipulation of resources, both current and future, will be matched against the returns available on the alternative mixes worked out. The total return on capital employed should also be assessed in current assets as well as on the basis of the future investment profile. Sufficient cash flow must be generated to maintain existing resources and build up new ones. Capital budgets should be framed for the period of the plan showing expected returns for each year. Projected balance sheets should also be cast for this period.

Non-economic objectives Subsidiary to the economic objectives are the non-economic or social purposes which a firm must set itself, e.g. security of employment, acceptable wages and working conditions and high standards of service to the public.

THE TACTICAL PLAN

The tactical plan spells out in detail how the strategic section of the corporate plan is to be set up and implemented. The tactical plan is sometimes called the operating plan in that it devolves the responsibility for seeing that the strategy is carried out upon various sections of the company. There are four main tasks in setting up the tactical plan. They are as follows:

1 ORGANIZATION PLANNING This is concerned with creating the structure with which the company's strategic objectives can be most successfully achieved. Obviously the restructuring necessary must be done with the least possible dislocation to operations and with the maximum cooperation from all employees. Management techniques such as management by objectives can aid this re-structuring.

2 MARKET PLANNING This is concerned with the development of the chain in line with the strategic objectives and its geographical implications are discussed in chapter 5.

3 RESOURCE PLANNING This deals with the budgeting and disposition of manpower, materials, services and cash flow in the short term, and the problems are dealt with in various parts of this book.

4 IMPLEMENTATION These tactical plans must be tied together and implemented. Corporate objectives must be broken down into unit objectives which should be communicated to individual managers in such a way that they will be motivated to give of their best. The inter-functional nature of long range planning requires that extra-functional groups be set up to coordinate planning. An appreciation of time economics would also be an advantage.

CONTROL AND CONTINUITY

In order that the corporate plans can be implemented fully, it is vitally important that controls be instituted which will provide sufficient feedback. Planned performance in corporate and in unit terms must be fully established and understood by those concerned and the actual performance matched against the plans, taking into account changes in the external environment, the validity of the original assumptions upon which the plans were based and all other changes in the company's total operation. This will allow the plans to remain flexible and dynamic and act as a check on their internal consistency. Flexibility allows short term *ad hoc* measures or alternative plans to be brought in as contingencies.

The plan should be thoroughly reviewed as a minimum requirement:

1 Annually to take account of the company's progress.
2 Whenever there is a distinct change in the company's market system, e.g. the merger of two large competitors.
3 Every 5 years to rectify basic objectives and make out a new checklist of strengths and weaknesses.[2]

SOME COMMENTS

The technique of corporate planning is not quite as straightforward a technique as a basic explanation given would make it appear.

For instance, there are two schools of thought on the setting of basic company objectives. One believes in starting from some idea of 'planned profit', while the other would base plans on 'the facts'. This simply means that, in one case, the corporate planner projects, say, a 35 per cent increase in profits over a 3 year period, arguing perhaps that the company should not be in that business if that scale of achievement is not practicable. In the other case, the corporate planner studies the strengths and weaknesses of the company *vis à vis* its environment first and *then* calculates what profit objectives can realistically be set. It can be argued that both methods are equally correct and equally logical, and the split is rather over means than ends. Both schools ask the key question 'How much better could we be doing?'[4]

Would-be corporate planners should beware of mistaking strategies for objectives. A firm such as J. Sainsbury which intends to have 250 supermarkets open by the end of the 1970's is expressing a strategy rather than an objective. It is important that a particular profit level is explicit in board members' minds (or even published) because of the danger of 'sub-optimisation' where one department's profit goals are out of step with the company profit objectives, thus endangering the corporate ends. Certainly, the long term planning concept does not fit easily into the normal framework of routine budgetary control and financial planning. The sharing out of responsibility for achieving profit goals among senior line managers is a cumbersome business if the central plan limits divisional or subsidiary management autonomy.[2] Even management by objectives is not necessarily of great help in this sort of situation which requires that unit rather than individual objectives should be set.

Any sort of planning can become a straightjacket and, as pointed out, a large amount of flexibility is required within the plan's framework so that speedy reaction can be made particularly to external changes. This sort of built-in flexibility should help management to react to unexpected challenges. One of the benefits of corporate planning is regarded as being the clearer sense of direction which it can give, if intelligently progressed. It must certainly cause management to rethink the position of their company within its environment, and anything which achieves this can be welcomed.

The time scale or horizon over which the company plans (perhaps 5–10 years) is important for several reasons. Businessmen are an impatient breed and often expect returns on investment to flow fairly quickly. Long range planning is a case in point. Expectations of speedy results are incompatible with the necessary time for planning to work through the system and produce returns. This has caused some disillusionment with planning modes and specifically with the concept of corporate design. Management style is often determined by time scales. In an entrepreneurial situation, for instance, there is a tendency for *ad hoc* planning arrangements to be set up to deal with particular situations, to the exclusion of long term requirements. In any event managers who are used to planning over a 1 or 2 year period find it hard to adjust to a longer time scale. There is an argument here for a concentrated education programme *before* long range planning is instituted to attempt a change in management style. In the few cases that this has been attempted it has apparently been quite successful.[5]

A corporate planning system should not conflict with an existing power structure. If planning is to be taken seriously the structure itself has to be changed. The attitudes and calibre of the chief executive, other directors and senior executives are crucial to the success of corporate planning which, without effective support becomes merely lip service and, as such, a waste of resources.

Anthony Thorncroft in a *Financial Times* article of 28 January 1969 summarised the main conclusions of a BIM Information Summary on Corporate Planning prepared by John Hewkin and Professor Tom Kempner. They are particularly apt as a summary of this section:

9

1 Long range planning should be company-wide and coordinated. Successful planning does not necessarily depend upon the establishment of formal processes. In large companies, however, an organised but flexible approach seems logical.

2 The scope of planning should be comprehensive. One particularly important aspect which is often neglected is organisation planning. This is often a difficult and delicate process, but if carried out intelligently is well worthwhile.

3 The development of specific strategic objectives within an overall framework of general company aims is essential to successful planning.

4 Plans should outline intended action in the long term and short term on a fully integrated basis. It can be very useful to break down the planning process formally into long range, mid-term and short term aspects.

5 Planning must be concerned not only with 'what is to be achieved' but also with 'how it will be achieved'. Figures are the end point of planning, not the plans.

6 Planning decisions must ultimately be the responsibility of executive management in their respective areas of operation, no matter to what extent the detailed work associated with planning is delegated to specialist staff.

7 Specialist planning staff can often be used in an advising capacity to executive management. Planning departments should be small, and 'empire building' discouraged. In addition to advisory work, it may be appropriate for their responsibilities to include the coordination of plans.

CASE STUDY

Let us take the case of a 150 retail branch company in the grocery trade, subsidiary to a large national group with interests in retailing, manufacturing and management services. Annual sales in 1970 were £2½ millions and sales over the past 5 years had just kept pace with price increases. Pre-tax profits for the grocery multiple had fallen from £72,000 in 1965 to £15,000 in 1970. Most of the branches were small and located mainly in secondary positions in old district centres in the North of England.

The holding company board, which had taken over the firm in 1968 but had not made further investment in it, were faced with the position that the return on net assets in their subsidiary had fallen to 3 per cent largely as a result of the fall in profits. The main board decided to call in a firm of management consultants to investigate the problems and suggest some sources of action. The consultants were to report findings direct to the chairman of the holding company.

CONSULTANTS' FINDINGS

The consultants (a team of three specialists headed by a senior) spent a period of 8 months in the subsidiary—not, of course, full time—and wrote several reports under the main headings of marketing, finance and company organisation.

Marketing In a report on the company *branches* it was found that:

1 20 per cent were making consistent losses of over 5 per cent and were incapable of further development.
2 A number of branches would be affected by redevelopment plans within 5 years and would have to be closed completely or resited.
3 Most of the branches were small counter-service units (less than 600 ft² sales area) and had a cluttered appearance. They were, in fact, poorly organised.
4 No uniform identity was apparent in the shops and what could be termed as 'personality' was not acceptable in terms of better retail practice.
5 All but a handful of the larger branches contained fittings which had been written off entirely and were therefore in need of some form of modernisation.

The *merchandise* report stated that:

1 The range of goods sold was too large and the fact that the ranges were generally common to all but the very smallest branches contributed to the clutter in the shops; it was estimated that some 85 per cent of lines contributed only 25 per cent to gross profit.
2 There was very little reasoned use made of selective price cutting but manufacturers' sales aids were much in evidence.
3 Stocks tended to be far too high in each outlet and with generally poor stockroom accommodation, the in-store clutter was intensified. A proportion of the stock in branches was out-of-date and thus unsaleable.

Finance The *financial* report stated that the accounting procedures of the company were faulty and that through wrong charging of gross margins and the levying of only 2 per cent notional rent on freehold properties (of which there were a number) the company was effectively in a break-even position. It was also found that payment of suppliers (many of which were local) was done on a haphazard basis and that useful discounts were being lost on one hand and that cash flow was being reduced on the other. Branch accounts were only prepared annually and were partially deficient on usable information.

Company organisation On the *personnel* side it was found that productivity in the branches was low (£50 per week per assistant) and as a result of over-staffing wage percentages were high (as much as 20 per cent in some outlets). Staff turnover exceeded 200 per cent in some shops and the overall staff turnover in shops was in excess of 100 per cent. Staff morale was low, partly due to an uncompetitive wage scale. A training programme was under discussion but had not been implemented.

At senior levels, a number of elderly and unsuitable managers were in authority.

In summary, this was a classic case of a badly run company whose weaknesses could be encapsulated thus:

1 Lack of positive leadership and motivation at senior levels, largely due to insufficient knowledge of the current situation with consequent inability to define objectives.
2 Poor communication at all levels, partly resultant from (1).
3 Lack of planning (e.g. in management succession and development areas).
4 Lack of urgency, again partly resultant from (1).

Having detailed the weaknesses of the company the consultants listed the strengths which were:

1 40 per cent of shop sites were freehold and about half of these were quite valuable.
2 An enthusiastic and able middle and lower management was employed.
3 The resources of a group were available.

CONSULTANTS' RECOMMENDATIONS

The consultants produced in conjunction with the main board a corporate plan for the subsidiary (and were, incidentally, later asked to produce plans for the group).

The overall objectives were to be as follows:

1 To increase return on net assets to 20 per cent by 1975.
2 To increase trading profit (before any group charges and without acquired profit) by 1975 to £150,000.
3 To increase market share to £4 millions by 1975.
4 To create a better staff environment and conditions.
5 To create an acceptable corporate identity.

The strategy by which this would be achieved was outlined as follows:

Increase profitability 1 By resiting, closing, modernising and reorganising the chain's shops with a view to controlling a chain of 100 outlets of at least 800 ft² sales area each. It was recommended that one of the retail development team at group level be seconded for 2 years to advise on detailed courses of action and carry out an approved plan, responsible for this performance to the subsidiary's new managing director.

2 By instituting central (group) buying procedures as far as possible and reorganising the relationships with local suppliers.

3 By setting up a new stock control system for branches using the group's EDP capacity. The target was to double stockturn rate by 1973. The throughput per line would be monitored through quarterly stocktaking and a variety reduction would be implemented as soon as sufficient data was available.

4 By employing a new accountant with retail and EDP experience who would reorganise accounting procedures with a view to using the group computers for wages, payments and receipts. He would also be responsible, in conjunction with general management, for setting up a new accounting system for the shops which would incorporate sales, expense and profit budgets.

5 By reorganising the firm's personnel and training functions (a replacement was recommended for the existing staff manager) with a main view towards raising staff productivity and improving staff morale. An organisation chart was to be produced with the agreement of the chief executive which would indicate clear lines of responsibility. The personnel manager was to review staff to ensure that staff were of the right calibre, skills and experience and in the right numbers, appropriately organised to carry out the tasks and meet the objectives.

Increase market share 1 By relocating and improving branches in those areas where higher sales were regarded as possible, and by taking into account competition.

2 By searching for new products with higher margins.

3 By setting up sales promotion schemes allied with selective price cutting for certain lines, based on suppliers' discounts.

4 By acquiring local grocery businesses with a substantial return in growth areas.

Improve staff environment 1 By paying higher wages (this would be possible with a smaller number of larger, modernised units).

2 By staffing to scientifically assessed establishments in each branch (it was recommended that the management services department of the group carry out some work measurement investigations).

Corporate identity   By building and fitting standard units designed to project a new corporate identity; this was to be reflected in all aspects of the company operation. (It was recommended that initially the group advertising department would investigate this problem and produce designs; it was felt that to go to a design consultancy at this stage would be too costly.)

IMPLEMENTATION

It was decided that the reorganisation of the company would be financed by either selling completely or selling and leasing back the freehold shops owned, and by a subvention from group for the balance (the group would also be supplying some personnel and services). The managing director of the subsidiary was to be responsible for the implementation of the plan and would report on progress at regular intervals to the group chairman.

All staff members were told of the plans and asked for their comments at several special meetings. The progress of implementation was regularly communicated to staff as it took place.

MANAGEMENT TECHNIQUES

The following section describes some of the management techniques which may be useful in a retail firm.

CORPORATE STRATEGY

Corporate planning   See previous section.

Decision theory   This is the study of how analytical methods can be applied to the process of making decisions. In most cases the theory is applied in circumstances where there is a degree of uncertainty and resultant risk. Many business decisions are taken without complete knowledge. Computers are now used much more frequently for calculating the risk–gain elements between alternatives. In coming to a decision the probability of certain events occurring is taken into consideration and a *decision tree* compiled. This technique is highly sophisticated and depends to an extent on the subjective assessments of executives in the compilation of input and screening of output. Decision theory is most applicable to investment decisions where there are a number of alternative calls on resources.[6]

Model building   This involves producing input data for a computer which incorporates, say, the present state of a company's marketing with further information on possible changes in the firm and in the environment. Models are usually designed for specific purposes and can estimate the effect of market shifts and government, competitive or in-firm policy changes. Models may provide optimum solutions to the way a company's strategy should be directed. Total retail company models would incorporate the financial, marketing and personnel aspects of a firm and offer them for evaluation in line with the input data. Work on total systems of this kind are not at an advanced stage, but when they appear the process of decision taking for long range planning purposes will be much more simplified.

Management by objectives · John Humble, regarded as the leading authority on management by objectives in Great Britain has described the technique as: 'A dynamic system which seeks to integrate the company's need to clarify and achieve its profit and growth goals with the manager's need to contribute and develop himself.'[7] Although the technique is rightly preoccupied with achievement and objective rather than with task, it is not a substitute for corporate planning, but may be part of it. It is primarily concerned with the spelling out of company objectives in individual and unit terms; the manager knows and understands his own targets and how they fit into the corporate plan because he personally sets them.

By clarifying with each manager the *key result areas* of his job and setting *performance standards*, a management guide can be produced, with *information controls* so that individual objectives can be set and achievement monitored. These are agreed by the manager with his superior and form a short achievement (rather than task) orientated job description. The objectives outlined in the guide should, of course, be related to department and company objectives. Additionally, a *job improvement plan* is agreed which suggests how targets can be raised to improve overall performance. A *performance review* monitors actual achievements against objectives, while a *potential review* identifies the strengths and weaknesses of the manager himself and suggests possibilities of either improving his own performance within the existing job or of promotion. The essential factors which must be present to enable the system to work at all are an organisation structure which is unambiguous and gives the individual the potential to perform, and an information system of a detail and frequency sufficient to allow the manager to take quick corrective action. For smooth continuation, further back-up is required in the form of a training programme, and a management succession plan. These should provide the motivation along with rewards for achievement.

Some companies have reported tangible benefits from an MBO programme (e.g. Barclay's D.C.O.) and there is no doubt that the technique can have a sustained morale building function. It is absolutely essential, of course, to have the wholehearted approval of the board of directors for such a programme and useful (although this is not always recognised) to induct board members. It is also vital that the system should be one of self-control rather than imposed control, but this depends largely on the relationships in the organisation before the introduction of the system: an authoritarian management will lead to an authoritarian system.[8] On the other hand a self-control system in an organisation which is weak or which has not fully participated in the scheme at the most senior levels may run into difficulties in keeping MBO rolling and effective.

There are other problems. The setting of objectives between manager and senior poses problems of strategy, i.e. a compromise has to be reached as to the realism of the objectives agreed. Again, the greater the importance placed on the attainment of objectives the more they will become ends in themselves. Unit or group objectives may have to be set to stop sub-optimisation by one manager to the detriment of his inter-dependent colleagues. The key result areas in some positions (particularly in staff) are unquantifiable, which does not of course indicate their lower priority. The pressure on attainment of objectives may force the manager to concentrate on those results which are measurable to the detriment of other areas. MBO is essentially a short to mid-term device for backing up a corporate plan. Other techniques may have to be introduced latterly.

INFORMATION FLOWS

Management by objectives   See previous section.

Costing systems   These involve the production of standard costs in retailing for such expenses as wages, rent and rates and general expenses so that they may be fitted together in a budget along with standard gross margins and net profit. Standard costs can also be used for capital as well as revenue budgeting. The standards serve as control figures but one of the chief difficulties, apart from setting viable standards, is keeping them up to date.

Organisation and methods   This is a form of systems analysis where a company's administrative procedures are checked for efficiency and kept under constant scrutiny, using techniques such as cost benefit analysis. The aim of the O&M department is to see that the value of manpower is optimised at least cost to the firm, and the task of 'policing' the system embraces work and method study, the checking out of information flows, investigation of the best types of office machinery for routines and so forth. In the wider field of management services, O&M may act as a liaison between management and the EDP department where costs of data production can be crucial.

Computers   The use of electronic data processing and information retrieval systems have penetrated the retail industry to an extent comparable with many other activities.

The most important function that computers undertake in retailing is stock ordering and control, which should ideally be controlled by some sort of recording at or near point of sale. There are various forms of imput for such recording, one of the best (unfortunately not applicable to all types of merchandise) being the dual purpose punched card and price label, e.g. Kimball tags. Other 'off-line' systems include cash register coded tally roll readings into the computer and the transcription of orders on to punched cards or tape to be fed into the machine. Orders may also be scanned by document readers or visual display units which carry out the input function. 'On-line' systems transmit sale data direct from the cash register to the computer. If a viable system for recording transactions can be applied to particular merchandise, a stock control system can be set up for storage and retrieval in the computer. Efficient stock control depends very heavily on the reliability of data collected at point of sale. The production of this information may be costly and a study for a potential stock control system must take into account the cost of data collection and match it with the benefits flowing from reduced stockholding and depreciation. The computer can of course throw up slow moving and unprofitable lines and aid variety reduction. One of the most successfully utilised computers in a retail firm in Britain is that at Mothercare headquarters at Watford, but the system there is simplified by the use of Kimball tags and the comparatively small range of 800 lines. The use of an EDP system in companies with 20,000 lines or more would obviously be beneficial if a manageable and low cost recording of sales is possible. Another important use of computers in retailing is data output on branch performance which may incorporate sales, gross margins, main cost heads and net profit. Here management by exception becomes important because of the large volume of information created by a national chain of shops.

CAPITAL PROJECT EVALUATION

Discounted cash flow This popular but widely criticised technique of capital investment appraisal calculates the rate of return on a project and can be used for assessing alternative investments in retail projects. A study is made of the rate of return at which the original capital outlay is exactly equal to the 'present value' of the later cash (profit) inflow. The present value of the profit inflow is the amount of cash which would have to be invested (e.g. in a bank deposit) today at X per cent interest to be able, just, to pay £Y in 1 year's time, 2 year's time and so on over the length of the project. Taxation, investment grants and other factors are also taken into account. In other words, DCF measures the value of money as a straight investment against its value in a capital project. Because a bank can begin paying interest as soon as cash is deposited it is worth more than cash which may take several years to produce profit in a capital project. Unfortunately, like most capital appraisal techniques, DCF does not take account of the present decline in the value of money.

Conventional methods of calculating return on investment are dealt with elsewhere in this book.

PROJECT CONTROL

Critical path (network) analysis This technique is of particular use in controlling the planning and opening of a new branch and ensures that the various stages of the work are brought forward in correct sequence with the minimum delay and at the least cost. The CPA highlights those elements in the project which are 'critical', i.e. those whose timing and completion may affect the whole project. The network chart consists of a series of activities or events joined together by lines or arrows indicating the sequence with an estimated time allowance given to each. The arrows fan out from the initial order or decision and come together again at the completion of the project. The chart can be analysed by adding together the estimated times along each of the paths from job start to completion. One of these lines is called the critical path and is the line on which bottlenecks are likely to occur. Management uses the critical path line for main control. 'Float' time is shown for various phases of the project and this can be used for adjusting the implementation if any hold-ups should occur. A standard network can be produced for shop opening from the checklist in Appendix III, but it is a large and fairly complex one which is therefore not reproduced in this book. CPA can save time and money, conserves manpower and helps to keep target dates on schedule.

OTHER TECHNIQUES

Other management techniques are dealt with elsewhere in this book, notably retail market research, statistical forecasting and manpower planning.

SOURCES AND REFERENCES

1 *Corporate Strategy.* H. I. Ansoff. McGraw-Hill, USA, 1965.
2 'Do's and dont's in corporate planning.' D. Hargreaves. *Financial Times.* 26 September 1967.
3 'What the barrow boys can teach company bosses.' R. Heller. *Observer.* 28 February 1971.
4 'What is corporate planning?' *Economist.* 5 October 1968.
5 'The pitfalls of long-range planning.' B. Denning. *Financial Times.* 19 June 1970.
6 'How to use a decision tree.' G. Laing. *Financial Times.* 2 October 1970.
7 *Improving Management Performance.* J. Humble. B.I.M., 1965.
8 'A jaundiced look at M.B.O.' I. McGivering. *Financial Times.* 15 April 1969.

2
STRUCTURE PLANNING

It will be clear from the preceding chapter that the ideal management structure of a company should flow as naturally as possible from the agreed corporate strategy of that company. Once the strengths and weaknesses of a company, including the organisational ones, have been assessed, the firm's structure may be reorganised to meet the new corporate objectives. This may require the setting up of new departments and the recruitment of management talent, but it also requires that changes in the existing structure be carried out with the least possible dislocation to operations and the maximum cooperation from employees. Like the corporate plan as a whole, the new organisation structure must be 'sold' to employees. Throughout the changeover the corporate planner (whoever he may be, for example chief executive, head of management services or someone specially recruited) must see that relations between employees and company continue to be amenable throughout all phases. Some of this responsibility may be delegated to the personnel function.

he responsibility for operating the new structure plan once it is agreed and put into operation should be with the personnel department but this does not, of course, absolve senior management from the need to create the plan in the first place and see that it is being carried out correctly.

The existing structure of many retail companies does not necessarily match up entirely to their current objectives. This may be due to policies of merger or takeover which have created duplication of function or the need for new departments. One of the ideas behind corporate planning is to avoid administrative difficulties of this kind by planning out anomalies in the system.

The organisation structure of a retail company will depend to a large extent on the type of trading that it carries out. Because this book is aimed primarily at the multiple retailer, only the appropriate type of organisation for a chain operator will be discussed. The essence of multiple retailing is the dispersal of branches, each serving different catchment areas. This leads to problems of communication which would not occur if the retailer operated only one or two shops. The branch manager may feel to a greater or lesser extent, depending on the support of his supervisor or area manager, somewhat isolated. Not only does this situation compound the importance of training, but the man selected to manage a branch must be of a calibre sufficient to take on-the-spot decisions and show general initiative. Whereas on a factory floor a supervisor can discuss problems with his immediate superior and come possibly to a more ordered decision, a shop manager may not see his senior for several days and some problems cannot, of course, be discussed on the telephone.

Another problem is that some retail firms may not be large enough to carry the specialist departments like property and merchandising which can act as supports to the individual shop manager. The result is that some of this work, such as personnel selection, property maintenance and display will have to fall on the shoulders of the shop manager or his supervisor. We now go on to discuss the stages of planning in the organisation context.

THE EXISTING STRUCTURE

An organisation chart similar to that shown in Fig. 2.1 should be drawn up to outline the functions and relationships within the structure, and to see that every important task is carried out, but not duplicated. It is important, in conjunction with the creation of an organisation plan, to have job descriptions produced for each manager from executive directors downwards. The technique of MBO can help here. Ideally this work should be carried out at the inception of a scheme for corporate planning so that the forecasts for future growth are readily available, up-to-date and originating from the same base line so that they can be easily related to a new structure. A management audit is useful at this time: this means reviewing current management practices and operational policies to see how they fit into existing and future structures. Any weaknesses should be corrected within the new structure which may be more complex than the old due to the planned growth factor.

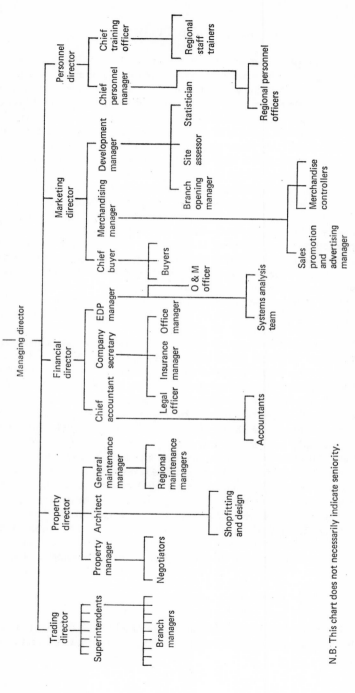

c

Fig. 2.1   A typical organisation chart for a retail multiple firm.

N.B. This chart does not necessarily indicate seniority.

THE MANAGEMENT INVENTORY

In order to plan a new structure successfully and forecast future management requirements, an inventory of existing management talent must be taken which will account for the education, experience, ability, interests and past performance of individual managers. In order to identify each manager's strengths and weaknesses, the above elements are matched against the man's salary, current responsibilities and potential. A gap may occur between his performance to date and his assessed potential, unless he is now occupying his last (most senior) post in the company, i.e. has reached his 'plateau of competence'. This gap can be filled, provided there exists potential within the individual for future development and consequently greater responsibility by training, further experience and/or promotion. The idea behind the management inventory is to identify personnel capable of filling the jobs outlined in the structure plans. Some of this work is made easier if there is an adequate and up-to-date personal record for each manager. Some form of reporting system (perhaps similar to that used in the Regular Army) of seniors on their subordinates could be used. A more sophisticated technique is job evaluation as used by Shell and other large companies. The three primary areas of job evaluation are accountability, know-how and problem solving.

Accountability isolates the results the manager must achieve and their impact, and how much freedom he has to achieve the end result. The know-how factor involves the amount of professional knowledge and management expertise required. The job may be inter-disciplinary (or not) with consequent problems of knowledge, human relations and motivation. Problem solving, the third element in job evaluation, outlines the requirements for identifying, analysing and solving problems in a particular *milieu* and the quality and degree of thought-work needed. All three areas are interrelated and are checkable for internal and external consistency. Each executive takes part in the evaluation of his own job (somewhat on the lines of MBO) which helps to increase his own awareness of function and responsibility. The evaluation has to be matched up with salaries and perquisites in order to come to decisions as to whether individuals are in the correct jobs. This technique's main disadvantage is that it is task rather than objective orientated (although the latter also has its own disadvantages, as has been pointed out).

FORECASTING GROWTH

The job and talent inventories must be carried out in the light of possible organisational changes resulting from planned growth. In retailing, growth can be quantified in terms of sales, number and size of units, geographical spread of branches and so on. Problems of retail growth may be tackled in several ways: an increase in the staff complement at head office to deal with increased paper flows, for instance, or the use of computers to carry out the same job, the revamping of supervisor's areas, the recruitment of more branch managers or training of existing potential. It is probable that several structure plans will have to be drawn up for the duration of the long term plan. The next section discusses some of these possibilities.

MANAGEMENT PLANNING AND DEVELOPMENT

RECRUITMENT

Many companies must rely on outside sources to fill management vacancies, particularly in a growth situation where too little attention has been paid previously to training or to organising properly the management resources available. External recruitment can be beneficial in that it provides a cross-breeding of experience. Many of the older middle and senior managers in the retail industry have stayed with one firm all their working lives and have thus become, perhaps, slightly blinkered as to the merits of their own company's methods of operation. On the other hand, massive external recruitment may bring some instability, particularly if a large part of the intake is of 'management trainees' who may leave if the subsequent training programmes are not satisfactory in any way.

TRAINING

If the correct identification of a manager's strengths and weaknesses has been made a training programme can be set up for him so that any gap can be closed and the manager's weak points strengthened. With the setting up of the Industrial Training Boards under the 1964 Act the whole problem of training within industry has been transformed. How effectively the grant aid system is being translated into trained or re-trained personnel has been the subject of much discussion, but with the increasing belief in cost effectiveness by successive governments, it is likely that the Boards will carry out their functions properly.

MANAGEMENT SUCCESSION PLANS

In order that the new structure of the company be matched by the available personnel, succession plans must be produced to slot personnel into their final niches at the appropriate time and replace retiring management. Table 2.1, which is set out as a balance sheet, shows the long term management requirements of a 200 branch retail firm over a 5 year period.

TABLE 2.1   Management requirements

Debit		Credit	
Estimated future redundancy		Current surplus	8
(branch closure)	20	Estimated rationalisation	
Present vacancies	6	benefits	5
Retirements	39		
Known leavings	4		
Probable extra wastage			
(based on past 5 years)	50	Estimated managements	
Requirements for expansion	60	requirements over 5 years	166
	179		179

Table 2.1, which includes head office management, is based on a structure which includes 200 shop managers, 20 relief managers, 20 area managers and 40 head office general and staff managers. The replacement rate per year for both head office and area/branch managers is thirty six and this is the figure the company must work upon.

Future selection will obviously screen job applicants to the standards required by the firm but job conditions, prospects and salaries must be competitive enough to attract (and retain) managers who are not only suitable for employment in the first instance but who will make a tangible contribution to company profits in line with the long range forecasts.

CAREER PLANNING

Once managers are employed by a firm career plans must be set up within the framework of the structure section of the corporate plan. This is part of the management development function which in larger companies would be carried out by the personnel and training departments. By giving managers the opportunity to take in knowledge and skills for their future positions (and also taking into account the man's personal ambitions) the company is building up a tactical plan for its organisation. Once the presence of a management development and career planning structure (and their individual prospects) is made known to managers their motivation, coupled with the training, remuneration and other factors which are built in, can be improved and thus help to ensure the retention of worthwhile individuals.

MANAGER'S HANDBOOK

Although not strictly concerned with the above, it is essential that an operating manual be produced in retail companies to give guidance to individual managers who may not see their seniors for several weeks at a time. This 'bible' will be concerned not only with the principles of good housekeeping but with the many other problems which beset retail branch managers today, e.g. the laws relating to property, sale of goods and theft. For excellent summaries on many of these subjects, see W. J. Philpotts' *Retail Business Administration* (Bibliography).

3
PLANNING IN PRACTICE

The preceding two chapters have touched on the rationale behind planning, but it would be mistaken to think that this is the end of the problem solving exercise. Indeed, it would simplify management decision taking if reason was as endemic in business as some writers on management subjects appear to assume; certainly reason is inherent in the techniques of management and policy formation. The real problems of management today, in the author's view, lie deep in the motivations of some senior managements who, when faced with reasoned alternatives in investment opportunities, take policy lines dictated less by reason than by personal foibles. The political nature of many board decisions has not been intensively studied, nor has the financial ignorance which sometimes takes its hand been subjected to scrutiny, although Robert Heller, editor of *Management Today* has let off a few rockets in his fortnightly articles in *The Observer*.

The simple lesson here is that incompetent management can ruin a company no matter what excellent control systems are initiated by middle management. If boards recognised the simple fact that they are effectively handling *cash* in their resource manipulation, some of the problems facing British industry could be if not solved at least ameliorated, to the satisfaction of stockholders, the government and the public at large.

Some of the influences currently at work in the retail field towards greater efficiency are now discussed.

26

SOME CASE STUDIES

Let us look specifically at a number of retail firms in various trades to see how they have tackled the problems facing large multiple operations today.

FINE FARE

The resuscitation of Fine Fare, the supermarket division of Associated British Foods, by Mr J. G. Gulliver who joined as its chief executive six years ago is one of the success stories of modern British retailing. From a 1965 pre-tax profit of £85,000, profits were approaching £5 millions in 1970. Group sales from a static £75 millions in the mid-1960's had by 1970 more than doubled.

The basic weakness of the business (which is made up of supermarkets, self-service and counter-service stores) in 1965 was a lack of planning. This lack made itself felt in the normal ways and was not helped by the over-centralisation of the chain. Development area planning was minimal and the over-expansion which occurred in the early 1960's was plainly on view all over the country: empty shells with a Fine Fare fascia, many of which never traded. The firm 'tried to do too much too quickly' said one retailer; 'they became the property developers' dream. They would lease anything.' But bad siting was only part of the story. Where Tesco had bought Fine Fare stores sales jumped substantially.

The over-centralised control which Gulliver took over had created a lack of direction at Welwyn Garden City (the head office) and in the branches themselves. Communications were poor as a result and morale was low. It was only to be expected under these conditions that management performance was indifferent and overheads too high.

There was also the problem of corporate identity, or lack of it. Somehow, Fine Fare never got its image quite right. Trading stamps were a large part of the problem. Garfield Weston, the group's owner, was forced to abandon stamps when Lord Sainsbury led the Distributive Trades Alliance into boycotting Weston's 'Sunblest' bread. With one marketing tool out of the chain's hands, Fine Fare had no reputation either for fresh high quality provisions (Sainsbury) or the rock bottom prices of Tesco, Pricerite or the then Victor Value. It has been argued that the group's name did not help its image having, as Anthony Bambridge of *The Observer*[1] put it, 'a Fortnum and Mason ring'. (Fortnums are, of course, part of the ABF group.)

Apart from anything else, Gulliver has brought a sense of continuity to Fine Fare, which was much needed in the early 1960's with the high turnover of branch management. The missing ingredient was indeed management: 'I took over a fantastically precious asset which is now beginning to realise its potential' said Gulliver in 1967. This is even more true 4 years later. Gulliver, as an ex-Urwick Orr consultant, introduced the disciplines of modern management techniques into Fine Fare. By scrutinising each section of the business, Gulliver isolated the weaknesses and set about correcting them.

The first priority was to halt the trading loss and to break even. Clear financial objectives were set for each part of the assets, branch by branch, and an assessment of the cash flow and working capital requirements produced. Branches were rationalised and the distribution system improved. Management by objectives was introduced which spelt out in management guides the formerly ill defined nature of many executives' jobs.

The EDP department is now geared to provide management information which has allowed regional decentralisation to occur within the framework of the corporate and unit objectives laid down.

On the marketing side Fine Fare has developed over 400 own brand products some of which already outsell proprietary brands by two or three to one. It is, however, the company's declared policy to limit its own labels to around 20 per cent of total sales so that the housewife retains her freedom of choice. Own brands of course engender customer loyalty and this will further be enhanced, it is hoped, by the work done on corporate identity which will affect 'every manifestation of the Group from store fascia to overalls, using the new corporate symbol and 'colours' (1969 Progress Report).

In the field of store operations, the group has embarked on a modernisation programme that by the end of 1971 has updated 300 supermarkets at a cost of £1½ millions. This is in addition to a planned opening programme producing 200,000 ft² of extra supermarket sales area each year. A computer study has recently been carried out to determine the best location in the stores for all the products that Fine Fare sells. The sales, gross profit and cash contribution of over 3000 grocery lines were examined so that each supermarket manager now knows the amount of space each product should occupy and where it should be on his store shelves.

WOOLWORTH

While the managing director of British Home Stores, Kenneth Mackenzie, has been quoted as saying that his chain has 'no obligation to be universal providers', the declared Woolworth policy is that its stores are 'the place where you can get everything'. Ten years ago this formula was highly successful. Not only was its profitability and return on net assets superior to any other chain in the UK, but it was a sought after share by investors and was held up as a model for siting and location by other retailers who, if they could afford the rent and rates, pitched themselves as close to a Woolworth branch as possible. Marks and Spencer has largely superseded Woolworth on most of these counts today and the severe dip in Woolworth pre-tax profit which became apparent in 1969 was continued through into 1971.[2]

Many theories have been put forward to explain this situation which caused a well reported uproar among shareholders who formed a ginger group early in 1969 because of static dividends (20 per cent for 8 years) and a poor showing by its shares on the Stock Exchange. The leader of the shareholders group, Mr Walter Shaw, made the point early on that £1 invested in Woolworth shares in 1960 would be worth very little more today, while the same investment in Tesco in 1969 would be worth £9·50.

The charge of complacency has been levelled at the Woolworth board, but one of the potent factors in the company's fall from grace must surely be the severe competition it has met from a large number of multiples who have, within the last 10 years, extended their ranges quite markedly and set up a strong competitive element. Tesco, Boots, W. H. Smith are only three firms which have expanded the number and average size of their outlets during this period.

Kelsey van Musschenbroek in a *Financial Times* article on 25 March 1969 suggested that the image of the company was not clear-cut enough, that too many things were being attempted all at the same time, that its trading-for-cash policy with suppliers was over-generous and that its 'home grown' executive board was bound to be inward looking because of the 52·7 per cent equity holding by the American parent company.

Let us discuss these theories in more detail.

1 *Image* Woolworth have for many years been selling a range of own brands, but there was still at the time of writing a proliferation of these ranging from household paints, through Delamere canned goods to Winfield for new lines. There was therefore no identifiable brand image such as St Michael. According to another *Financial Times* article on 4 December 1970 by David Walker, Woolworth is implementing a major corporate identity programme and changes are to be made in the company symbol, in the branches, in own brand merchandise and in staff uniforms. The scheme, it is estimated, could cost more than £500,000. Mr L. B. Sherlock was appointed in Autumn 1970 as director with particular responsibility for sales promotion and advertising.

2 *Over-ranging* Woolworth are presently pruning their massive range of commodities and several thousand lines have already disappeared. This is in line with the BHS programme, but Marks and Spencer are extending their ranges currently (so, of course, have Tesco, Fine Fare, Boots, W. H. Smith and several other chains). The pruning is being carried out scientifically, if conventionally, by reducing on slow sellers

and low margin commodities (there can be a danger in blanket range appraisal: one variety chain decided at a particular stage of its development to withdraw staple but slow selling food lines such as salt and flour from its food halls, but quickly reinstated them when it was discovered that housewives expected them to be there and deserted in droves). Woolworth is also trading up into higher priced merchandise and using selective price cutting.

3 *Trading for cash*   Woolworth argues that, although it may lose the financing advantages of credit, the 'cash on the nail' treatment for suppliers reinforces its buying power substantially; it is likely that this policy will remain.

4 *Internal board promotion*   This has certainly been a serious criticism of the company until recently, but the appointment of Mr William Beddow (an outsider) in the key financial chair may be pointing the wayt to the future.

5 *American control*   This is not regarded as being a damning indictment of UK Woolworth. As Kelsey van Musschenbroek points out in the article referred to: 'A good deal of the present retail revolution in Britain has its origins in the U.S.', Woolco being a case in point.

The company announced a major modernisation programme for many of its smaller stores in mid-1970, alongside the Woolco developments. One major strength of the chain is the large amount of freehold properties which have been estimated as being worth £200 millions, according to John Davis in an *Observer* article on 1 March 1970. These properties, unencumbered as they are, offer tremendous scope for capital financing by sale and leaseback or using them (as does Marks and Spencer) as collateral for raising loan capital for expansion and development. Twenty six stores were closed in 1970.

The general opinion is that if the present moves towards scientific management are successful the still great potential of the chain can be further unlocked, but that this will take some years. The most recent results have indicated a continuance of the downward trend in profits. The 1970 results showed a fall of 7 per cent to £34·5 millions with a sales increase of only 3·5 per cent. Margins held high at 10·7 per cent. It is felt that profits should have begun to rise in 1971 with the new management, the revamp of stores to a 'cash-wrap' operation and the extension of Woolco coverage. It is expected that wage costs can be cut by 15–20 per cent by this sort of action.

THE CO-OPERATIVE

As in most businesses, lack of success brings a plethora of reports. The Co-operative Wholesale Society has been reported on several times since

1958 when the Gaitskell Commission, among other recommendations, suggested a reduction in number of societies from 875 to 307. This report was followed by the Co-operative Union's National Amalgamation Survey in 1960 and the CWS Joint Reorganisation Committee report of 1965.

The basic problems of the Co-op in this country were:
1 An inefficient production orientated set-up.
2 A complex committee structure at all levels with all the disadvantages of democracy, particularly a lack of professionalism.
3 Too many societies, many with uneconomic units.
4 Lack of an up-to-date image.

This has been reflected in sales which had remained static at just over £1000 millions for several years.

Philip Thomas an ex-Fine Fare man was recruited in 1967 and began tackling the problems in an aggressive but conventional manner until his death in an air crash in 1968. His successor has carried on the work and the present situation can be outlined as follows.

A good deal of inefficient CWS manufacturing plant has been closed and investment has begun in more modern, better sited plants and warehouses as part of its rationalisation.

The CWS have now worked out a unified marketing scheme whereby retail prices, stocks, shelf allocation sales promotions and so on have been accepted by the Societies. There has also been a swing away from Co-op brands with the insistence that national brands be given a reasonable share of shelf space. A reverse trend to that with multiple supermarket own brands is foreseeable in that the share of sales held by Co-op brands will fall. A large amount of variety reductions has also taken place. Deep price cuts on selected lines have been backed by heavy television advertising.

The old committee structure has given way in many operating areas to a more formal line and staff structure and there has been a good deal of recruitment from outside the organisation. A number of important new recruits had, however, left by the beginning of 1971.

The number of societies has declined drastically, even since 1968 to somewhere quite close to that recommended by the various committees previously mentioned. A further rationalisation into 50 large regional buying groups has already started, notably with the creation of the North Eastern Society out of 31 previously separate societies. These regional societies, it is planned, will be served by 30 warehouses.

A corporate image has been created with the help of Lippincott and Margulies who recommended that the 30-odd food brand names along with the many more non-food brands be rationalised to the Co-op name. A new symbol has also been chosen. The 'Operation Facelift' campaign, mounted to modernise the movement's retail image is well under way. Half of the Co-op's 12,000 outlets were brought under the new logo by Autumn 1970 and the number of 3000 ft² supermarkets rose to 1340 by the end of 1970.

Within 12 months of some of these measures being instituted the Co-op's share of the grocery market crept up to 16·1 per cent. After a dip during tardiness over selecting Thomas's successor the trend was again upwards. The indications are that if all these plans are fully implemented that the Co-op should become much more of a force in the present highly competitive retail situation, although a further fall in profits was recorded in the 12 months to January 1971.[3]

CONSULTANTS

Retailing has now reached the stage in this country where consultancy investigations are likely to be beneficial. The increasing competition between firms in the same and different trades, the large scale growth of some retail companies, the pressure on margins and the general movement towards more technical modes of thinking among management have, among other things, created problems which are not necessarily surmountable by existing management. Coupled with this, there is a certain industrial *apartheid* between retail management and that in some other industries. Hence 'few consultants have been able to make much contribution largely because retailing presents particular problems which not only demand the normal armoury of management expertise but also a large measure of practical experience'.[4] How different *are* the problems of retailing compared with those in other industries?

There are certainly one or two unique problems in retailing; the others are matters largely of degree. Generally speaking—and this applies particularly to the high volume retail units which make up the majority today—the industry is plagued with relatively low and fluctuating gross margins and a cost profile influenced by a number of unusual features:

1 Labour intensive with extensive use of part time workers.
2 Higher than average accommodation costs per foot.
3 Relatively high pilferage and stock wastage.
4 Generally low unit value per transaction.
5 Large number of transactions per day.
6 Very uneven activity levels throughout day, week and season.

In practice, this means that any further pressure on margins is unacceptable, i.e. will produce an uneconomic return on investment. Further problems include the difficulty of distributing to each outlet a large number of lines further subdivided by size, colour and so on, controlling this stock within the branch and accounting for it. The majority of these problems can be either solved or improved by the use of certain management techniques which are common to many industrial operations.

It is interesting to consider the reasons given by firms for hiring consultants:

1 Sometimes the reason for poor company performance is particularly obscure and the consultant is brought in to put his finger on the trouble. Quite often the client will tell the consultant what they think is wrong and offer some solution.

2 Internal staff appear to lack particular experience or expertise that the consultants can give (the company should be aware of the skills and lack of skills of its personnel).

3 It may be more economic to use a consultant than to take internal staff off their own jobs, particularly when the latter are under pressure.

4 The need for arbitration between two departments on fundamental policy.

Consultants have additionally been utilised for 'political' purposes such as providing an excuse for a sacking or reorganisation.

Reasons for not hiring consultants have usually been that either the company did not need them or because, more cogently, they often lack the background knowledge of a particular industry to carry out their assignments effectively. This latter argument presupposes the 'specialness' of a particular industry or firm and ignores the fact that management's prime function is the manipulation of resources (cash, in the end) towards optimisation and in this they can be aided by certain management techniques. Sometimes company experience with consultants has not been happy. Provided that the consultancy firm is a reputable one, a failure of an assignment can almost invariably be blamed on the client. A weak board, who dimly realise that they themselves are the basic cause of a company's problems, may rationalise the situation and present the consultant with a brief on some other peripheral problem. A concise and adequate brief is essential for the consultant in any case and so is a full understanding on the part of management (and consultant) of exactly why the assignment has been given. It is also important that each board member concerned be totally committed to the consultant's brief. Lip service in matters of this kind can do much damage to the value of the assignment.[5] Robert Heller states quite rightly that 'the proper use of outside experts is as rifles aimed to pick off specific identified targets'.[6]

Chapter 1 gives an illustration of the type of job a consultant would do if he was invited by a retail company to make an investigation and recommend a course of action to improve the company's current position.

Professor Tom Lupton of the Manchester Business School poses three test questions for potential recommendations:

'Will it pay?'
'Will it work?'
'Will they work it?'[7]

The client must pave the way by a systematic approach to the problem to get over the obvious initial disadvantage that the consultant probably does not know the industry involved.

FUTURE SHOPPING LOCATION TRENDS

There has been a good deal written recently about the changes which are likely to occur in the provision of shopping facilities in Britain over the next few years. Much has been said about traffic pressures on urban cores and the need to rethink shopping location in the light of these pressures. Certain innovations have appeared as a possible solution to this problem, notably the Woolco/GEM type centres and the banning of traffic from some shopping streets during peak shopping hours. Retailers themselves are attempting to press forward with further ideas but have been baulked in many parts of the country by local authorities.

Let us look, firstly, at the retailer's case. In the supermarket sector the general trend is towards peripheral or out-of-town development. Tesco in 1968 took the view that potential during the 1970's was more likely away from town centres. As part of this strategy the company began searching for sites which would give between 60,000 and 100,000 ft² of selling space with parking for 1000 cars. In 1969 after a visit to the United States Sir Jack Cohen returned with renewed enthusiasm for one stop shops, ideally sited on the outskirts of urban areas. But he also stated that the preliminary applications his company had made for such single storey supermarkets had been turned down because the areas selected had not been designated for shops. Fine Fare has been looking for units in the 20,000–50,000 ft² range and have already opened some in peripheral locations, e.g. in Aberdeen. Sainsbury have opened suburban branches in Coventry (Bell Green), Luton (Bury Park) and Bristol (Bedminster) which, although not true out-of-town locations, bear the stamp of the company's current thinking. Mr T. A. D. Sainsbury, the director responsible for property matters, envisages a strict demarcation between the locations of convenience and comparison goods shops.

Supermarkets and other food shops should not be located in town centres but 'closer to the homes of most people'.

Very large supermarkets have been opened quite recently, however, in the centre of Croydon by both Sainsbury and Tesco and so there still appears to be hope for the town centre yet as far as its food shopping complement is concerned. Sir Jack Cohen did mention at the Croydon opening that this would be the last town centre Tesco department store.

Woolworth, through their Woolco Division, planned to open 20 stores by the end of 1973 in out-of-town or suburban locations such as those at Oadby (Leicester), Castle Lane (Bournemouth) and at Thornaby-on-Tees (see page 37) but the current opening rate is only one per year. Associated Dairies (Asda) have plans to extend the ex-GEM operation which they took over in 1966, these developments to be under the Asdaqueen Superstores name.[8]

A few other multiples have so far expressed a desire to move out of town or at least into the suburbs. Department stores, however, have been engaged in a relocation or branching programme for some years. A number of leading department stores in the centre of towns have been announcing very disappointing results recently. Finnigans the former Manchester department store moved to Wilmslow some years ago, thus precursing the new movement out of city centres. Anderson and Mac-Aulay in Belfast built a junior department store called Supermac $3\frac{1}{2}$ miles south of the city centre in 1964. Gamages set up a branch in Romford (but have since sold their store), Dickins and Jones in Richmond and Selfridges in Ilford. John Lewis are opening a branch in the new Brent Cross centre at Hendon (but are also opening a new store in the St James' Square development in central Edinburgh). The Parly 2 complex at Versailles with 100 shops also contains branches of several Paris department stores, including Printemps and Prisunic. According to a survey carried out on behalf of the Harrods division of the House of Fraser Group, for every suburban resident who shops in the West End of London stores, two are staying away and hoping to find their merchandise at local stores. James Beattie the Birmingham store opened in Solihull where a new shopping precinct was being built. Management said with regard to the traffic problems in central Birmingham, '(the resite) was clearly necessary and clearly it is paying off'.[9] On the other side of the coin, Debenhams who were originally going into the Brent Cross development decided not to proceed because 'it would have taken too long to make a profit'. But Marshall and Snelgrove (Debenhams) have closed their branches in Birmingham and Leicester. Other recent developments include the joint Sainsbury–Boots project to build a large store at Bretton, one of the new neighbourhood areas making up Peterborough. A sign for the future, perhaps, has been the attempt by Wheatsheaf Investments and the French company Carrefour to make several applications for hypermarket developments in England. One, at Telford, has been, at the time of writing, successful.

Let us look, secondly, at the local authorities' views on out-of-town centres. For some time, the statutory planners have put forward two reasons for being unsympathetic to this type of retail development. One is that the present and planned investment in conventional town centre and suburban shopping areas is so large that any peripheral shopping complex (perhaps of the hypermarket type) would ruin the trade in existing shopping centres by syphoning off large potential expenditure; the other is that much rate revenue would be lost from existing shops through this drawing off of potential sales. Birmingham, for instance, has a capital debt of £300 millions because of the investment in the central road system and improved amenities carried out to counter the choking of the city centre by traffic in an effort to retain trade in the high value central area shops. The city has in addition attempted to strengthen the power of its central core by allowing the Bull Ring and Birmingham Shopping Centre developments to take place, along with some other shopping redevelopment in the Corporation and New Street areas. According to the developers (Laing) the Bull Ring development became profitable in 1970, after 7 years of trading. In Liverpool and Leeds, for example, peripheral district centres have been planned to provide convenience goods for the local catchment populations. There is, in fact, a large vested interest, indeed inertia, in prolonging the existing retail structure, an interest which may not be borne out by the economic facts as interpreted by retailers and described previously. It is easy to be sympathetic to local planning committees, but there is some doubt that their efforts to improve the communications in town centres are going to be successful in the long term because of economic forces and because of the 1968 Town and Country Planning Act.

The 1968 Act (see Appendix I) has discarded the old rigid zoning system under which, for instance, shops could not be built in certain classified areas, and the Department of the Environment is now enpowered to ask local authorities to draw up more flexible 'structure plans' which will indicate both the growth areas by economic category and the likely location of their development. Local government boundaries are to be redrawn and the Department has advised that these structure plans will be submitted by groups of local authorities, whereas before local government boundaries did not necessarily bear any relation to catchment area boundaries. Further guidance has since been given to planners by the Department of the Environment and the National Development Organization.[10]

A few other retailers appear to be enthusiastic about these developments. Dorothy Perkins, Bata Shoes and Lex Garages have taken concessions in Fine Fare out-of-town supermarkets and the Bournemouth Woolco development which takes up some 70 per cent of the £1 million Hampshire Centre, has been joined by old established Bournemouth quality food store Williamson and Treadgold which moved from its old site in the centre of Bournemouth 'because we believe that the future of food shopping is where you can park your car'. Other tenants of the Centre include Currys, Millets and two major banks.

Anthony Thorncroft comments in an article in *The Financial Times*:[9] 'So far we have heard too little from the housewife on the type of shopping facilities that she prefers.' Unfortunately, she does not know in many cases. One survey, however, suggested that over 44 per cent of housewives prefer the inconvenience and strain of High Street shopping against 7·5 per cent who liked the out-of-town centres. In a campaign for a hypermarket at Chandlers Ford, Hampshire, most local housewives did not know what a hypermarket was. After the distribution of 20,000 copies of a coloured explanatory news-sheet and a request for reactions, the 2000 replies showed that 68 per cent of housewives were in favour of a hypermarket for their area.[11] It is obviously impossible to draw firm conclusions from this sort of data. More powerful research into the effect of the Thornaby Woolco superstore has been conducted by the Manchester Business School's Retail Outlets Research Unit. This investigation revealed that the Woolco was not operating as a store with a large catchment area but as a local shopping centre which had probably damaged local corner shops more than anything else. The guidelines for hypermarket development laid down by the Department of the Environment state that acceptable plans would be 'on sites which offer good access, which are appropriate for the full range of commercial and social provision of a district centre and which are open to no other major objection on amenity or other grounds'.

MERGERS

A number of mergers have occurred in retailing over the past 5 years and it is quite certain that there will be others during the next 5. Mergers are, of course, of many kinds, the most common in retailing being of the horizontal type which involves the linking of companies at the same stage in the productive process, e.g. two retail firms selling in the same or complementary markets. We now discuss some of the general problems of merging and then go on to look at one or two actual mergers in the retail industry.

The reasons for a merger must be quite clear to both companies involved, although the suitor company is likely to have different reasons

37

for seeking or considering a merger than the bride-to-be. A possible list of reasons for retail firms to indulge in mergers:

1 Buying markets (including branches and distributive networks).
2 Eliminating competition.
3 Buying as a defensive strategy against future competition (safe-guarding future markets).
4 Buying management.
5 Diversifying for profit and strength.
6 Buying under-utilised assets.

If a corporate plan exists it will have to be rewritten to accommodate the new situation, although under the strategy and tactics outlined in the plan the possibilities of certain mergers may well be mentioned, if not their full implications.[12] A full investigation of the firm to be taken over, and of its strength and weaknesses, must be made in a retail situation under the headings:

1 Finance.
2 Marketing.
3 Management.

1 FINANCIAL CONSIDERATIONS

A company to be taken over must be fully investigated with regard to its accounts and its financial soundness. An investigation should go into the historical background of the company, taking into consideration its profit, net asset value, share price performance and dividend, capital commitments and so on before a decision can be made as to its suitability for merging. It is possible that the ROCE may be low which could indicate an under-utilisation of assets, checkable by similar company performances. It is also possible that certain assets can be profitably liquidated under a rationalisation of resources.

2 MARKETING CONSIDERATIONS

The market spread both in products and geographically must be investigated to see whether it would fit in easily with the approaching company or would require pruning. Some of the branches may not be financially viable as individual units but this would not necessarily come out at this stage. The basic requirements for a merger under this heading are that the company is reasonably compatible on a marketing basis once it is merged. Key pointers are overall market share and category market share and the geographic dispersal of sub-markets.

3 MANAGEMENT CONSIDERATIONS

Management must be fully assessed *on both sides* of the merger to point up any possible incompatibility or serious antagonism and, more importantly, the joint managements' quality matched against the new situation. The performance of the company to be taken over will, of course, reflect on the management available. There is little bonus to be had in creating sinecure positions for surplus staff, particularly board members.[13]

Once the various investigations have been completed it will become clear whether a basis for merger exists. It may be that a definite synergical situation exists (this means that through a combination a greater return will be produced than is achievable through the separate parts) but this can only be appraised by matching up combined resources, forecasting ROCE and comparing them with the return under the separate situations, a difficult exercise. If the merger would not only be beneficial and acceptable to both sides but would be workable, the next task is to produce an integration plan (which may be made up in advance for this sort of eventuality). One of the most important factors during the integration is to have total commitment to it all down the line in both companies. This requires not only a communication system which will keep employees in the picture as to each stage of the merger, but a formal education programme, basically to dispel fear of the unknown (rather than fear of change). Everybody must know what is to happen, why it must happen, when it will happen and what the result will be to themselves. Communication must cover not only individuals but organisations who will be in frequent contact with the merged company, e.g. suppliers, customers, agents, trade associations, trade unions, local authorities and any others likely to be affected.

It often appears that the benefits accruing from particular mergers are accepted with lesser regard to the disadvantages. Some mergers which have taken place, not necessarily in the retail trade where options are to some extent limited, have been 'ill-conceived, ill-planned, badly carried through and are to some extent weakening the industrial structure rather than strengthening it'.[12] There are the early disappointments where, through inadequate groundwork, over-valued stocks in the balance sheet have to be dealt with or the taken-over company's accounting conventions have to be tackled. More fundamentally, the new management may be ill prepared for the transition period during which the two companies actually become a corporate entity. Directors and senior executives taken on from the merged company, having sold their interest, may have lost their drive. Procedures must be set up not only to appraise the managers of their new role, but to guide them into unlocking the benefits inherent in the merger situation.[13]

Some companies have required to bring in outside consultants after acquisitions in order to have the problems sorted out. It is useful before the merger or acquisition is finalised to consider whether independent advice should be used to resolve points of difference or even to set up a checklist for integration and a revamped corporate plan.

Let us now look at one or two mergers which have occurred in the recent past. Boots the Chemists began integration with Timothy Whites and Taylors in May 1968. Of the 600 shops in the latter group 315 were selected for conversion to branches of Boots and processed at a rate of one per day. Seven further branches which were next door to Boots shops were incorporated with them to make larger premises. There were 94 Timothy Whites shops which were either too small or surplus to requirements which were sold. There were, additionally, 132 already trading as houseware shops only (no pharmaceuticals) to which a further 98 (including some Boots branches) were to be added to form the nucleus of a chain of hardware shops trading under the Timothy Whites name. A stock inventory based on the best of the existing Timothy Whites and Mence Smith houseware and selected merchandise from the larger Boots department stores was to be selected for the new chain.

By the end of March 1971, 198 Timothy Whites branches had been opened, a rate of progress rather slower than that predicted by the Boots chairman at the time of his annual statement in 1969. By March 1970 it had been agreed that a further 20 Timothy Whites shops would be set up in new areas, making a total chain strength of 250 by March 1971. 'If this chain is as successful as we believe, we shall expand it nation-wide as quickly as suitable properties can be acquired' said the chairman in his statement for year ended March 1970, adding 'although in its early days the sales performance of the new chain so far has been most encouraging'.[14]

The houseware and chemist operations are now being controlled in two distinct chains each with its own management and methods, the rationalisation of each chain having been successfully accomplished. The closure of nearly 100 small Timothy Whites branches has reduced volume but should contribute to future profitability. The development of the Boots chain has, of course, continued with the opening of 50 new branches in 1969/70.

Further cost savings were made in the coordinating of the Timothy Whites buying merchandising and distribution with the Boots group. Some property was sold off as a result. Timothy Whites branch ordering has now been put on to the Boots computer and the time scale for this was given as 12 months, which included the reorganisation of the six main Boots warehouses. Boots branded merchandise has been put into Timothy Whites shops and this should further reduce unit costs at factory level.

Boots have dealt with the merger in a predictably efficient way, although the integration between two chains with overlapping ranges and in the same type of location does not present the difficulties of some corporate marriages. With the Boots retailing skill the benefits are fairly obvious. At a purchase price of £37 millions (a P/E ratio of 28) the acquisition was cheap for Boots if not for other retailers. Boots have returned around 20 per cent on net assets for several years, against a 1967 Timothy Whites return of only 11·6 per cent. If it is possible to produce the Boots return from the Timothy Whites assets the purchase P/E ratio for the latter drops to 16, a much more viable proposition. If the Boots expertise is transmitted to Whites, the merchandising and location strategy should pay off.[15]

Another recent but much smaller retail merger was that, also in 1968, between Tesco and Victor Value. When purchased for £8½ million in shares Victor Value was running at a small loss. The purchase was treated on the basis of acquisition rather than on merger accounting and because the net assets of Victor Value were worth less than 25 per cent of the price paid, the balance had to be treated as goodwill in a situation where the goodwill was relatively valueless. On a straight financial basis then, it looked as though Tesco had paid well over the market value for Victor Value. But Tesco in its continuous expansion programme was anxious to secure extra sites and further branch management personnel.

A number of Victor Value branches have since been closed and their trade transferred, as in Orpington for example, to a large new Tesco supermarket. Some have been converted to Home 'n' Ware outlets but in all cases the Victor Value name has been removed from shopfronts (ending any vestiges of the goodwill element). Many of the 280 Victor Value branches were small in any case. Hyman Kreitman, Tesco's chairman and managing director stated at the time: 'I'm sure it (Victor Value) can be made profitable. How much and how quickly, I can't say.'[16] The problem is to squeeze Tesco-style profits out of the Victor Value asset. A very massive closure of the latter's branches (which has not occurred) would have reduced the profit potential, even at Tesco's level, substantially. Additionally, an asset must obviously be identifiable after integration so that its real (rather than forecast) profitability after rationalisation can be monitored. An apparently synergical situation could occur merely through more profitable use of the suitor company's original resources.

It is interesting to note two contradictory statements in connection with the necessary speed of integration. Willoughby Norman of Boots declared in his annual statement of 31 March 1969 that: 'Speed is the essence of this exercise in order to obtain the advantages of the acquisition as early as possible.' Conversely, Adrian Cadbury, managing director of Cadbury–Schweppes[17] stated that: 'There are only a few people in a company who can sort things out and they can't move too quickly' and 'only now (nearly two years after the merger) do we know what we want to do.' This seems to underline the need for the sort of pre-merger investigation and planning mentioned previously in this section.

The reasons why firms sell out has not been discussed, but the offer price is probably one of the major factors, possibly coupled with lack of apparent potential, dwindling of interest and/or profit motive and the approach of the proprietor's retirement age without management succession.

In summary, here are some examples of merger patterns which should *not* be taken as being the exclusive or prime reasons for the mergers:

Buying markets: Mothercare–W. J. Harris (pram shops).

Retention of markets: Ranks Hovis McDougall–Merry Miller Bakeries (London).

Buying sites: Boots–Timothy Whites and Taylors.

Extension of development area: J. Sainsbury–Thoroughgoods (Coventry, etc.).

Buying distribution networks: J. Menzies–Wymans.

Eliminating competition: Birrel–McColl.

Buying management skills: Tesco–Victor Value.

SOURCES AND REFERENCES

1 'How Weston's White Elephant got out of the red.' A. Bambridge. *Observer*. 2 April 1967.
2 'Woolworth the sleepy giant.' J. Davis. *Observer*. 1 March 1970.
3 'The C.W.S. problem' and 'What's on at the Co-op now.' K. van Musschenbroek. *Financial Times*. 22 January 1969 and 27 July 1970.
4 *New Ideas in Retail Management.* Edited by G. Wills. Staples Press, London, 1970.
5 'What industry thinks of management consultants.' H. S. Taylor. *Financial Times*. 26 February 1969.
6 'Calling in experts.' R. Heller. *Observer*. August 1970.
7 'McKinsey's blueprint for change.' M. Dixon. *Financial Times*. 15 January 1969.
8 'Out of town shops start to pay.' K. van Musschenbroek. *Financial Times*. 31 October 1968.
9 'Planners thwart more out of town.' A. Thorncroft. *Financial Times*. 26 November 1970.
10 *The Future Pattern of Shopping.* N.E.D.O. H.M.S.O. 1971.
11 'The selling factories.' A. Road. *Observer*. 31 January 1971.

12 'Checklist for mergers.' D. Hargreaves. *Financial Times.* 23 February 1968.
13 'Avoid the pitfalls in mergers.' A. Campbell. *Financial Times.* 23 July 1969.
14 *Boots Pure Drug Co. Ltd. Annual Statements* for year ended 31 March 1969, 31 March 1970 and 31 March 1971.
15 'Seven league Boots.' J. Davis. *Observer.* 19 May 1968.
16 'Tesco shops around.' A. Bambridge. *Observer.* 19 May 1968.
17 'Bournville starts to move.' A. Thorncroft. *Financial Times.* 25 February 1971.

4
DEVELOPMENT AND PROPERTY FUNCTIONS

We have seen the important part that marketing plays in the corporate planning and development of a retail firm. The two main aspects of retail marketing are the merchandising function and the development function. As explained more fully in chapter 5 these two functions are not mutually exclusive, the basic difference being that the merchandising department plans and implements the total buying and selling operation of the company while the development department deals with individual shop performance.

DEVELOPMENT FUNCTIONS

The main functions of the retail development department are:

1 To plan and implement the development and extension of the chain's branch operation in the long and short terms.
2 To analyse branch performance figures so that guidance on future development can be given to both line and staff management.
3 To collate and disseminate market information to retail line and staff management.

The first two functions are strictly connected with the objectives of the company and its strategic plan, but the department should be viewed as a staff management service rather than as a line function. The development manager should not be in a position to finalise any plans for expansion nor finally to decide improvements to existing shops. Because line management have to operate the shops, their views should override, in normal circumstances, those of the development manager whose prime function is to advise courses of action. The final arbiter in any clash of views should, of course, be the retail or trading director.

By using the language of management by objectives, eight key result areas are readily identifiable in the retail development manager's brief:

1 To create and update a development area plan.
2 To select sites for new shops and resites for existing shops.
3 To advise on the acquisition of new retail businesses.
4 To produce shop profiles for new and existing shops, in line with the agreed company image.
5 To control the implementation of the opening of new shops and refits of existing shops.
6 To research into and advise on means of improving the sales and profitability of existing shops.
7 To set up capital expenditure budgets.
8 To collect, hold and make readily available all the market information required for planning purposes.

He is aided in this by a number of specialists whose functions are discussed later in this chapter. Let us examine more closely what is entailed in these eight areas of performance.

1 DEVELOPMENT AREA PLANS

An up-to-date knowledge should be maintained in the development department of the following.

Population Trends over the whole country with particular reference to those areas where it is felt that successful branches can be operated. Very detailed data on population is available from the decennial *Censuses of Population* which break down local authority population figures into ward and parish complements; comparative information from previous population censuses is also included, and the 1971 census should be fully published by the mid 1970's. In 1966 the first quinquennial Census of Population was taken on a sample basis and this will further aid market planners. The decennial census contains a great deal of further data on socio-economic groups, country of origin, number of owner-occupied houses, age group and sex analysis, occupation and industry of informants and so on. A further useful (annual) publication is the Registrar General's *Annual Estimates of Population* which updates the main census information by the use of local Registry

Office information. Similar estimates are compiled annually for Scottish local authorities and for Northern Ireland.

Local and national planning Under the 1968 Town and Country Planning Act (which applies to England and Wales only) local planning authorities now produce *Local Plans* which consist of a map and a written statement. *Local Plans* are part of the larger *Structure Plans* and these and other documents (as detailed in Appendix I) will be available as they are produced at local council offices. Local newspapers normally report on planning proposals, but perhaps the best source of this type of information is the Multiple Shops Federation fortnightly *Planning Bulletins* which give condensed reports on all published local planning proposals.

Shopping environment Shopping centres are continually changing, not only due to local planning but because of decisions taken by key multiples to site, resite, extend, modernise or close their branches in a particular vicinity. Shopping centres new and old can be transformed in their potential by a Marks & Spencer opening, a rather more common occurrence today now that this firm has embarked on a moderate programme of new store building. Personal shopping habits change, too, albeit much more slowly. It is probably more true to say that shopping habits follow changes in the environment and shoppers themselves rarely create a new situation. Speaking quite generally, there are certain long term changes in shopping habits which are too well known to describe here, for example the movement towards more car usage for shopping, the increasing purchase of refrigerators and deep freezes and the consequent reduction in the number of times certain classes of people shop per week. One of the most recent reports dealing quite exhaustively with this aspect of shopping has been *People, Shops and the 70's* written by Jennifer Tanburn and published by Lintas, the Unilever subsidiary.

Competitors' activities Obviously, any change in the level of competition will have an effect on the trading of some retailers and it is useful for the development department to be fed with such information directly from the areas affected. This can be tackled by asking the branch manager to indicate in his weekly report what trading changes have occurred since the last report.

Updating the plan Information upon which can be based a system of updating the development area plan comes basically from two sources. Firstly, data collection involves the development department in monitoring official information sources such as those provided by central government agencies such as the Department of Trade and Industry, the Department of the Environment, the National Economic Development Council and so forth, local government agencies such as local authorities and new town development corporations, and private sources such as the Multiple Shops Federation, the trade and national press. Secondly, the firm's own retail branches can provide a great deal of information.

The development plan must, of course, be framed within the context of overall company objectives, while still taking note of changes in the external environment. It is possible that these two facets of development could clash and environmental changes in themselves could necessitate a change in detailed company objectives.

2 NEW RETAIL SITES AND RESITES

The retail development manager is charged with the task of selecting sites for new shops and resites for existing shops in line with the requirements of the retail development plan. This he will do by making market surveys based on property information supplied to him by estate agents and others and will report on his findings to general management and/or to his director.

He is also required to make sales forecasts for new branches and this will involve a cost appreciation which will show whether the particular project is viable or not. Performance of new branches will then be monitored to see whether they match up to the budgets. Close liaison is necessary with the estates department and this contact is discussed in more detail later in this chapter.

3 ACQUISITIONS

The development department will additionally be involved in collecting information on existing retail businesses which it is thought could be incorporated in the chain. Although the estates department would make a formal offer for a business, the calculation of the offer price is the responsibility of the development department. The department would be required to evaluate not only the means by which the business on offer could be rationalised into the existing chain, but to calculate what return on capital investment could be produced from existing assets having regard to cost savings which could be made once the business was purchased.

4 BRANCH PROFILES

Each branch in a chain has what can be called a 'profile' with five particular ingredients. One of the requirements of a national retail chain is to iron out individual differences between branches where possible and attain standards of uniformity throughout, having regard to local market

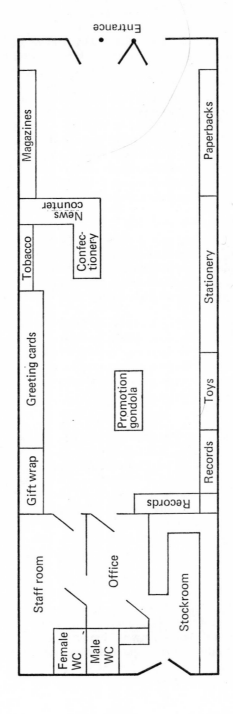

Fig. 4.1   Plan of a newsagents shop.

differences. By pinpointing these elements within existing shops the firm can gain a better idea of the identity it is searching for and the exigencies dictated by capital spending. These five aspects of branches are as follows:

Layout In some retail companies every branch has its own idio-syncrasies and the in-store layout often expresses these peculiarities. Some chain store branches are L- or U-shaped because of the presence of other retail company shops on the store frontage. Retailers by and large require squared-off shops without odd corners and returns because of the problems of shopfitting, maintenance, staffing and security which oddly shaped units create. The following two chapters discuss in more detail possible requirements as to shop dimensions, and if these can be made standard, a standard shop layout can be formulated showing the approximate display allocations for each broad category of goods, cash registers and the positions of departments, gondola and other free standing fixtures and the positions and sizes of stockroom, rest room and other ancillary areas. A sketch of such a layout plan is shown in Fig. 4.1. The National Cash Register Company and certain retail firms use models of fittings which can be placed on a graphed shop plan so that the various permutations on a layout theme can be worked out. This is particularly important to small multiple self-service food shops which may not be able to secure squared-off units of the size they require for particular market areas.

Fittings and shop front Once a chain is in a position to order bulk supplies of fittings, a catalogue of units should be produced, showing each fitting numbered such as to facilitate ordering for new shop projects. The production of prototype fittings may take some considerable time because of the experimental period during which the fittings are actually tested under operating conditions in selected shops. Once a satisfactory design has been lighted on production of bulk orders can begin, but there is little merit in making continuous changes to fittings because the cost savings achieved through ordering long runs may quickly be whittled away. The appearance and functional qualities of shop fittings are important parts of the image which the retailer may wish to project.

The shop front, too, expresses an image of a company and therefore careful thought must be put into its design. There may, of course, have to be slight modifications made to shop fronts to satisfy local planning bye-laws. For instance, all illuminated shop names in central Edinburgh have to be white in colour.

Ranging The actual fixing of the components of a range to be stocked in certain branches is the responsibility of the merchandising manager working in conjunction with operating managers. But the decision to stock whole categories of commodity (e.g. tobacco, swimwear, delicatessen lines) in a particular branch is recommended by the development manager and his staff who will have carried out a market assessment for the new shop soon after it has been contracted for, with the proviso that the site will produce an acceptable net profit because of its location. Market variations will cause the sales and gross profit participation for each class of commodity to be different for many shops, although the object of a multiple chain is to achieve as homogeneous a commodity profile as possible.

Variety chain stores grade their branches into four or five range types, depending on the size of the store which should, of course, be related to its market potential. Smaller branches are physically incapable of carrying either full ranges within each commodity class or even, in some cases, whole classes themselves. Some large supermarkets carry wet fish and delicatessen departments and the development manager must forecast sales in these departments and build them into the sales participation for the branch. This will obviously mean reducing the percentage participation for other commodity classes carried. Data on sales and gross profit participation can be obtained from an analysis of existing branch performance and these results applied to similar market situations, assuming that the property purchased is large enough to carry all the lines in the correct priorities necessary.

Operating costs   Here again, a budget for the operational cost of a new branch can be worked out by referring to actual costs of wages, shrinkage and general expenses in similar branches, i.e. in similar turnover bands, unit sizes and markets. The higher the sales of the branch the lower, generally speaking, become the percentage of each cost as a percentage of total sales. There is little merit in comparing the operating cost profiles for a counter service branch and a self-selection branch because the wage cost percentage is likely to be rather lower in the capital intensive shop; again, there is the higher risk of pilferage associated with open displays. Rent and rates percentages are a known factor in the breakdown of operating costs, but another important aspect of working out a profile is to estimate the gross margin available from sales once suppliers have been paid. The gross margin varies considerably from trade to trade and may be below 20 per cent in some supermarkets and newsagents' shops and over 50 per cent in catering establishments, jewellers and furniture stores. The actual mix of commodities carried will also alter the overall gross profit; tobacco, with a general mark-up of about 10 per cent can have a considerable effect on margins if the participation of this commodity in sales is high. This depressing effect can be intensified if the already low margin is reduced by retail price cutting. One large supermarket chain's average margin suffered quite substantially after it introduced cut price cigarettes into its branches.

Return on capital A simple formula can produce a return on invest-ment in a shop:

$$\frac{\text{Net profit}}{\text{Capital invested}} \times 100$$

The problem of defining capital invested in a shop is fairly straight-forward. It embodies two basic aspects, i.e. wholesale cost of average stockholding and cost of fixtures and fittings. Both capital items are subject to depreciation and the actual figures used in the calculation of ROCE should be the written down value of stock and fittings. In most retail trades it is probably academic to depreciate stockholding for pur-poses of return calculation. If, however, there are a number of slow moving lines which have to be sold off at a reduced price the deprecia-tion should be taken into account during a stock audit to determine the capital tied up in this particular asset. It has been argued that because of high stock turn some companies can work on a nil capital for stock and therefore stock should not be treated in this way. This is particularly true in the food trades.

Freehold properties are sometimes assessed as capital, but a rather unbalanced ROCE can result if property is treated in this way on an individual branch computation of return on investment. Many retail firms insist on a minimum of 20 per cent return on capital per annum and this is near the actual rate for the more efficient retail firms. One would not normally expect this sort of return on property, although the situation is made somewhat complex by the appreciation which often occurs on property values. This capital appreciation is taken into account by quinquennial property valuations. A more equitable method of calculating ROCE is to rentalise the current value of the property and therefore treat it as an operating cost. Currently, a superior covenant would produce about 6 per cent on a sale and leaseback operation, although some retail firms in order to service their capital more profit-ably do themselves charge interest and depreciation on their freeholds.

A further method of capital project appraisal is given in Appendix Xa. This method can be refined by the use of DCF Tables.

5 OPENING OF NEW SHOPS AND REFITS

A further function of the retail development department is to control the implementation of the opening of new shops and refits in existing shops.

The first requirement for carrying out this task successfully is the creation of a shop opening schedule (which can be usefully translated

Trade	Week comm. 24.4.70	Week comm. 4.5.70	Week comm. 11.5.70	Week comm. 18.5.70	Week comm. 25.5.70	Week comm. 1.6.70	Week comm. 8.6.70
Builder and Plasterer	Floor screed	Walls, ceiling, back area, and ceiling retail partitions		Frieze and ceiling (back area)			
Shopfitter		All back shop partitions ceilings and frieze groundings		Light trough, shopfront, fascia, back area doors and facings, etc., unit fitting			
Electrician		Wiring installations back shop area		Retail installation, ceiling light fittings, etc.			
Heating Engineer			Trunking installation		Heating unit installation		
Plumber				Water heaters			
Arcade Terrazzo					Terrazzo forecourt ingoes and fascia		
Glazier				Glazing shopfront			
Ceiling Fitter					Retail ceiling area		
Painter				Frieze and ceiling retail	All back shop areas and finishings retail		
Floor Covering						Floor tiles back area and retail	
Polisher						French polisher	
Industrial Cleaners						Cleaning	

Note: Site programme will commence 27 April and finish 12 June (i.e. extra week in hand).

into diagrammatic terms by use of critical path analysis). Before the actual work on the new branch or refit begins a pre-planning schedule or checklist is a useful tool for the development manager and his staff. This describes the stages through which a shop property must go from initial inspection of the unit and its market by the development team up to the handover by the shopfitters and the organisation of shop opening. The pre-planning schedule is contained in Appendix II.

At the pre-planning stage and up to completion of shopfitting and handover to the merchandisers, very close liaison has to be maintained with the property or estates department of the company. One of the most frequent reasons why new or refitted branches do not open on time is because either the building or the shopfitting of the unit has fallen behind schedule. It should be the responsibility of the estates manager or his subordinates to see that structural and fitting work is carried out to an agreed schedule. Many builders and shopfitters provide such schedules which can be copied to the estates department or kept for inspections on the site. Obviously the development department will not accept a new or refitted branch from the estates department until it is fully completed and acceptable to the retail operation (the director or general manager responsible for the trading in the branches). A copy of a shopfitting programme is shown in Fig. 4.2.

It is, of course, essential that a firm handover date of fitted shell be given by estates to the trading activity as soon as possible because this will allow stock ordering, recruitment, advertising and so on to be programmed. It is occasionally useful to provide a buffer of 1 or 2 weeks between completion of fit and commencement of stocking to allow for hold-ups which may occur due to shortage of labour or materials. These are sometimes unavoidable in the best regulated shopfitting businesses.

It is likely that small alterations will have to be carried out after the shop has been handed over but these should be of such minor nature that they do not require the handover to be delayed. It is useful to allow 2 or 3 months of actual trading to occur before tackling these minor problems, some of which only come to light when the shop has been 'run in'. Such is the pressure on many retail estates departments that it is often necessary to have all the modifications carried out at once to save time and cost, and the development manager, the trading manager and the estates manager may organise a site meeting with the shopfitters some time after the shop has opened to discuss the problems personally or through subordinates on the site.

A further function of the development department is to monitor sales and general performance in new and refitted branches once they are open. This should be carried out at least for a full trading year and ideally until the branch has attained its planned sales and profit targets. Such information, particularly if broken down into departments or

53

commodity sales, is a useful check on the location of the branch and its general layout. It is, of course, difficult to isolate these factors from the management competence, stock range and other elements in branch performance.

6 IMPROVEMENTS TO EXISTING SHOPS

Chapter 7 deals in depth with this particular aspect of retail development, but the department in this context is expected to research into and advise upon means of improving the sales and profitability of existing shops. Under this general heading are the matters discussed below.

Performance monitors Existing branch performance should be kept constantly under review in order that the development manager can advise on any improvements in location or internal layout. It is useful to graph sales on a moving annual total basis.

Experimental shops It is possible that a retail firm may wish to experiment with new layouts in certain shops and the development manager would be expected to suggest suitable shops for this. He might also advise on the components of such experiments and carry out the implementation control and monitoring of them with the agreement of senior line managers. The purpose of such experiments should be clarified before agreement on this form is reached and budgets should be prepared by the development department as to capital costs and profit return.

Improved retail methods All new methods of retailing, particularly those most applicable to the retailer concerned, should be studied by the development manager who should report as necessary. This may involve attending special courses, visiting shopping centres at home and abroad and studying the trade press.

Liaison with other departments The development manager must maintain close liaison with all retail operating departments, and with the merchandising and estates departments so that everyone is in the picture. Much of this liaison can be carried out through a formal series of regular meetings or at *ad hoc* sessions between executives. The development manager should be responsible directly to the marketing director or chief executive and should, of course, report to him through a formal system and/or as necessary.

7 COMPILATION OF CAPITAL BUDGETS

Although each general manager may make suggestions as to the details of a capital investment budget for shops, it is useful for the development manager to coordinate this information for board approval. This is distinctly useful when the retail function is controlled by two or more general managers, each responsible to the divisional director or chief executive. The make-up and control of capital budgets is discussed more fully elsewhere. A simple form for presenting these budgets is shown in Appendix IX.

8 MARKET INFORMATION

The development department should also carry out the function of collecting, holding and making readily available all the market information required for planning purposes. The department may also be required to carry out original research, possibly into the markets for new products.

This function may involve the department in setting up a central filing system for the activity, but basically it involves creating an index of all useful sources of market information including trade and government publications and competitors' data. An index of required company (internal) information including that from the estates department is also useful.

ORGANISATION STRUCTURE

A possible organisation structure for a development department is given in Fig. 4.3.

THE DEVELOPMENT MANAGER

As head of the retail development department, the manager should be directly responsible to the marketing director and thus to the board of directors. His function falls into the staff rather than line management as he controls a support group or service to the retail operation as a whole. Figure 4.3 illustrates the sort of structure which would be appropriate for the larger retail company, one perhaps turning over (at retail prices) something over £100 millions per annum and operating anything from

Fig. 4.3   An organisation structure for a development programme.

100 large stores up to 1000 smaller units. The department is also likely to be dealing with up to a net 10 per cent per annum increase in outlets and about the same increase in sales (not including refits, resites or extensions). The task of the development manager and his departments has been outlined already in this chapter and this particular specialisation is vital to the successful growth of a retail firm in that it takes from the operating managers the main task of improving the company's performance in the many ways open to a retail firm.

The manager himself is likely to be a graduate, possibly of economics, with considerable experience in the retail field, including some line management. He is therefore likely to be at least 30 years old and capable of commanding a salary (at current prices) of at least £3000 per annum. The salary scale is unlikely to be in excess of £5000 per annum except in the very largest retail firms.

Directly responsible to the development manager are the following section heads, not necessarily mentioned in order of importance.

THE SITE ASSESSOR

This man (or woman) is concerned with the following aspects of the work of the development department:

1 To make estimates of sales performance at (say) 1, 3 and 5 years for new retail shop projects and to make similar forecasts for any other projects such as resites, extensions and refits which are regarded as being major.
2 To make recommendations on marketing policy for a new shop project in terms of the broad commodity ranges to be carried, the possible sales mix and the estimated market share.
3 To produce operating costings and return on investment appraisals.
4 To secure information from the local authority concerned on the planning envisaged which is likely to affect the location in the future. This would include population forecasts, enlargement of shopping centres and so on.
5 To be responsible for collating files on planning in the development area.

The site assessor is likely to be numerate and literate with a general retail background, including line management experience. It is essential that he have been in retailing for at least 2 years because the specialised skills of estimating sales performance in new shops (in the author's view) cannot be gained outside the retail industry. The further experience required to carry out the task successfully, such as a grasp of local and national planning problems, the structure of a local authority and the whereabouts of source material can be gained through working either with an experienced retail site assessor or under the firm direction of the development manager who should have as part of his own basic experience some knowledge of site assessment. This position, which would be regarded as a crucial one and therefore commanding some seniority in the department, would not be given the status of a section (i.e. with subordinates responsible to the assessor) unless the expansion and development programme of the company is particularly heavy. The assessor would be able to secure assistance from other section heads in the department as necessary.

BRANCH OPENING MANAGER

The function of this manager is to see that the opening schedule for new shops, refits and relays is adhered to and implemented. In some retail firms he is merely referred to as the 'store opener' who may receive specialised help from merchandisers of various products. With the status of a manager, however, he is required to carry out certain other important functions, such as ordering stock. A brief summary of his job is as follows:

1 STOCK ORDERING AND DELIVERY He must ensure that all stock for new branches is ordered and delivered on time and that all additional stock required for refitted or extended branches is also available. He will obviously progress stock delivery through the merchandising manager or controller, although the initial ordering should be done in conjunction with the development manager, merchandising department and operating management.

2 STOCK CHECKING AND PRICING All new stock is priced by the branch opening manager or staff seconded to him prior to its display.

3 ESTABLISHMENTS He must see that the new branch is staffed to the requirements agreed by operating management. This may also entail checking that initial wages are available to pay new staff; initial till floats can also be dealt with at the same time.

4 SHOP EQUIPMENT He must ensure that all sundry equipment, e.g. cash registers, staffroom furniture, commodity signs, etc. are provided in line with the official list.

5 MERCHANDISING He must ensure that displays of merchandise are completed in line with the timetable for branch opening.

6 OTHER ASPECTS This manager is not directly concerned with the completion of shopfitting which is the concern of the estates department (see following section), but he must ensure that all other aspects of the completion after handover are up to date and finished on time. He may also be required to keep accounts of his

purchases of sundries if these are bought locally (for convenience) and not stocked by the estates department. These purchases should, ideally, be dealt with by the property accounting system.

Depending on the heaviness and exigencies of the branch opening and refitting programme, this manager may be called upon to progress relays in existing shops where the development manager, in conjunction with line management has decided to reorganise an in-store layout.

Because the manager is likely to be someone of experience in branch management his advice on many aspects of the development department's work may be valuable, particularly on branch layout, design of fittings, promotional ideas and so on. His capacity in this respect should be purely advisory, however, and he should not without the permission of his senior alter agreed layouts, order unauthorised merchandise or arrange special promotions.

The appointment should be regarded as a fairly senior one with the possibility of it being a section head position (see organisation chart) in larger firms. The subordinate merchandisers would be experienced in particular commodities and would be expected to give advice to the shop planner as to departmental location, size of display allocations and so on. They should not be confused with merchandise or stock controllers who are part of the merchandising department.

SHOP PLANNER

The function of the shop planner is, within the confines of the plot selected for a new branch, to draw a plan of the layout which will be based on information given him by the site assessor and statistician; these two later would liaise to produce space allocations for various departments in line with the requirements of the particular market. The shop planner should be a draughtsman with some experience of drawing up plans for retail shops; he would be responsible for seeing that, on plan, available space was being used efficiently and that the cash points, aisle widths, etc. were correctly placed and of acceptable dimensions. It is likely that he would receive a shell drawing from the estates department and, after the layout plan had been agreed by the development and general managers, the completed plan would be returned to property department, listing the fittings to be used in the finished shop. If possible he should also have some shopfitting experience and would represent the development department during the shopfitting phase, making checks on dimensions, types of fittings actually brought in by the shopfitters and so on. This would be particularly important if the property department did not carry a shopfitting and design section and all work was contracted out. In this case, the shop planner would work in with the branch opening manager at project handover.

STATISTICIAN

Although not essential, a person either qualified in or with a broad knowledge of statistical techniques should be on the staff of the development department to process the mass of statistical data which flows from a retail chain operation. The techniques of statistical analysis mentioned in this book are quite simple but much more sophisticated techniques can be applied to retail figures, particularly in smoothing out seasonal fluctuations in sales, in extrapolation and in elementary sampling procedures. Much of this work can be computerised, however, and allowing for the workload which the firm puts on its own machine or on its bureau, this extra information may be secured quite cheaply. Certainly there should be in the department both a statistical and filing clerk to collate and monitor data for the departmental manager and his staff. This collection would include general marketing data.

The statistician would also be involved in the preparation of sales and profit budgets, analysing the sales of merchandise groups and establishing proportions attributable to price and volume increases in total sales.

Some of the very largest retail companies have fragmented the functions described above into numerous sub-units, some of which may come under the trading or merchandising departments or divisions.

THE PROPERTY DIVISION

We discuss in this section how the property division or estates department can best serve the interests of the trading function and the company as a whole. The functions of this department are essentially those of service and support in carrying out the agreed retail development plan for the company and may be discussed under the following headings:

1 Acquisitions.
2 Disposals.
3 Surveys.
4 Planning application.
5 Project planning and control.
6 Costing, budgeting and accounting.
7 Design.
8 Maintenance.
9 Other statutory duties.
10 Asset management.
11 Liaison.
12 Control of stocks.

I ACQUISITIONS

The acquisition of new property, whether it be new sites or extensions on existing sites, is the lifeblood of an expanding retail company, provided that the acquisitions fall within the limits of an agreed plan of development and that the new found property is capable of profitable use.

The bulk of new properties, for most firms, are channelled through estate agents and the estates department should possess firm instructions from the development department as to the type of locations required, the frontage and internal dimensions, the maximum rent payable and so on. These and other details should be outlined in the development plan so that both the estates department and their various agents have a proper brief to work to. Agents receive an expansion list on the lines of that shown in Appendix VI. Once the development department has a detail on a site which appears viable, sales and profit forecasts can be made and, on the basis of these, the estates department can begin negotiations to purchase the property.

Lease details must be scrutinised for clauses which require special attention. These may include user clauses, assignment rights, subletting rights, right to make alterations, additions and improvements and right to change the use. In addition, length of lease, review clauses, repairing and insurance obligations, service charges, rent free period and so on should also be screened either by the estates manager or a conveyancing expert. The estates department is also responsible for publishing and circulating to agents notes for agreement on leases.

2 DISPOSALS

As part of the development plan, which should include elements of rationalisation and loss reduction, there may be a number of branches within a chain which require to be disposed of. Again, the estates department either circulates agents with the details or advertises in the trade, local or national press.

3 SURVEYS

The estates department institutes surveys of properties to be acquired to estimate the value to the purchaser as opposed to the rent or price asked. Surveys should also show any defects in the property which would entail expense in reinstating it. It is obviously essential for proper surveys to be carried out before signing a lease or buying a freehold. Either the estates manager or a surveyor retained for the purpose may carry this out.

4 PLANNING APPLICATION

The estates department must make all necessary approaches to the loca authority on planning matters. This requires the submission of all plans for acceptance by the authority, including shopfront and fascia, external signs, staffroom accommodation and so on. The department is also responsible for checking the local plans and Register of Planning Applications for anything which might affect the site in the future.

5 PROJECT PLANNING AND CONTROL

When the estates department is satisfied that the conditions of contract are acceptable to the firm and that the survey has been competently carried out and is also acceptable, the actual exchange of contracts takes place and the property is then either owned or leased by the retail chain.

The project is now in train and the task of the estates department is to plan and control it up to handover to the trading activity. A rough costing based on standard costs will already have been done by estates for the benefit of the development department. After the shop layout has been agreed (including all services) the next step is to put the project out to tender which may mean contacting three or four shopfitters with specifications. Some building work may also be required. Once a tender has been accepted, the estates manager will begin planning the job and delegating the functions. Many shopfitters produce a programme (see Fig. 4.2) which should then be organised to allow any building work and wet trades at the commencement of the project and a handover date fixed so that the shop opening programme can be pre-planned. It is important that some leeway be given in the fitting programme to allow for shortage of materials and labour and on a 6 week fit a shopfitter often adds a week or 10 days to allow for eventualities.

The estates department must produce a complete programme and progress it through so that handover is not delayed. The department may employ regional property managers or surveyors who can visit the site for meetings and generally oversee the progress of the fit.

Some sophisticated estates department use critical path analysis to control progress on projects, but whatever the control methods, it is the responsibility of the estates department to see that the timetable for handover to retail is adhered to so that the branch opens on the advertised date. The department is responsible for checking finished work and can refuse to accept it on behalf of the retail firm.

Each project, whether it be acquisition or refit, should be phased into the total development programme for the year (and in line with the agreed budget) so that the estates department is not faced with an overload programme at certain periods. It is vital, too, that the number of projects contained in a budget is kept within the ability of the estates department to plan and control effectively. Estates should at agreed intervals supply to operating management a review of all work in progress with reasons for delay in the programme. Figure 4.4 shows a programme of property development.

Major Works Schedule

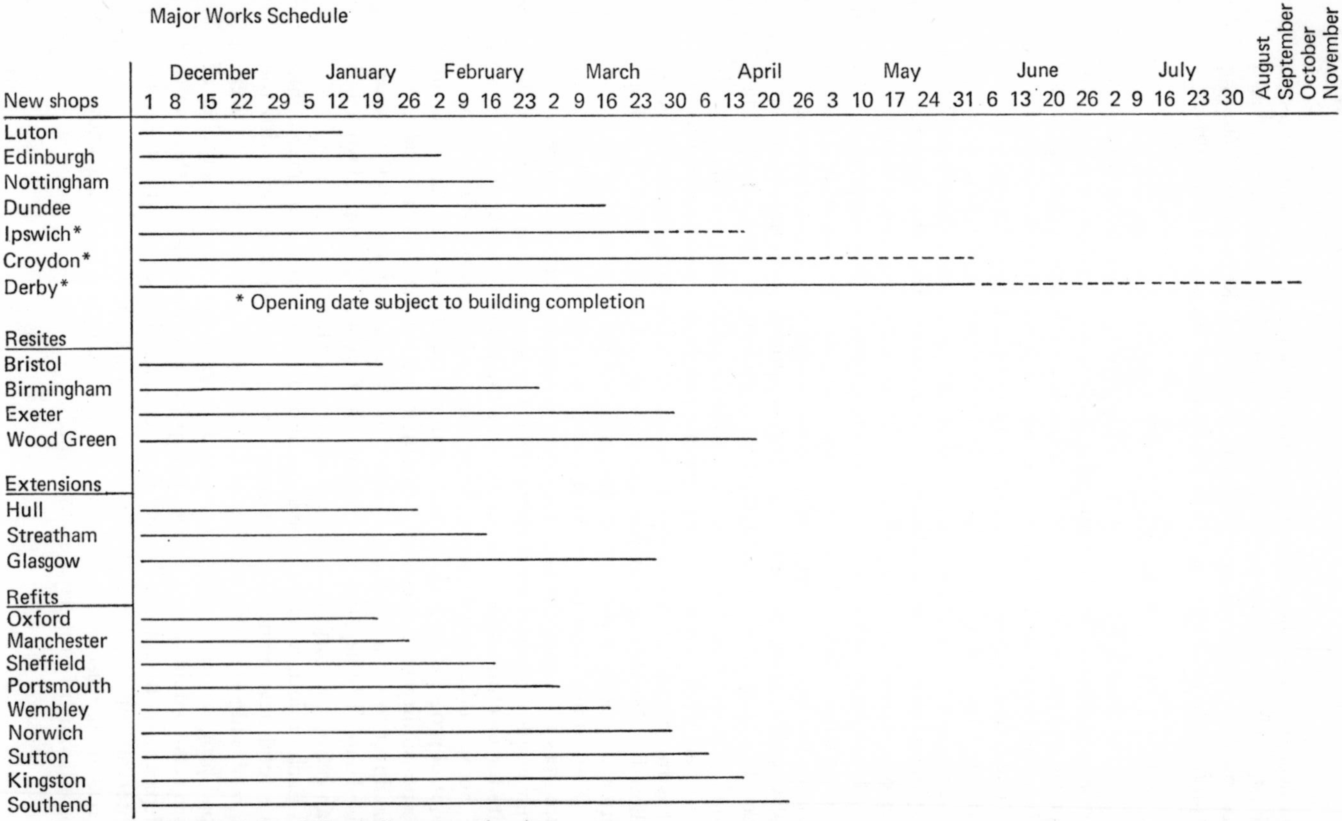
December
January
February
March
April
May
June
July
August
September
October
November
1 8 15 22 29 5 12 19 26 2 9 16 23 2 9 16 23 30 6 13 20 26 3 10 17 24 31 6 13 20 26 2 9 16 23 30
New shops
Luton
Edinburgh
Nottingham
Dundee
Ipswich*
Croydon*
Derby*
* Opening date subject to building completion
Resites
Bristol
Birmingham
Exeter
Wood Green
Extensions
Hull
Streatham
Glasgow
Refits
Oxford
Manchester
Sheffield
Portsmouth
Wembley
Norwich
Sutton
Kingston
Southend

N.B. End of each line indicates opening date

6 COSTING, BUDGETING AND ACCOUNTING

The estates department should be able to cost out in approximate terms the price of a project. This will mean that a schedule of standard costs per unit of fitting or per square foot of sales area must be worked out. These costs must be accurate and up to date enough to match against tenders received: costs are continually rising and budgeted project costings must be reliable enough for this purpose. The estates department should have as one of its objectives to see that tender prices match with actual bills as they are presented. The department should have the expertise to isolate the factors which have contributed to any cost disparity and be prepared to argue it out with the shopfitter, architect, structural engineer, quantity surveyor or whoever is responsible.

The framing of capital budgets should be done by the development department. This department is responsible for calculating the return on investment and any deviation from the budgeted costs will obviously affect this calculation. The actual control of the budget should be in the hands of the estates department which should also carry a general accounting system of some kind, separate from other systems in the company in order to deal with invoices for payment and so on. The estates department should frame *maintenance* and replacement budgets.

7 DESIGN

The division's architectural section must see that adequate drawings are made of the building firstly for the guidance of the shop planner and secondly for the guidance of the shopfitters, builders and so on. These drawings should be to accepted scales and should show dimensions, position of wall fittings, lighting, heating, floor covering, wall and ceiling finishes, colour schemes, materials, shopfront and fascia, stockroom and staffroom facilities, stair positions, etc. All later modifications and amendments should, of course, be notified to all concerned.

Estates should produce a catalogue of fixtures and fittings, each fitting being coded and priced (the latter as part of the standard costing procedure). Fitting design should be updated according to experience under operating conditions and new merchandising methods. All shopfitters should work to these approved designs which must first have been agreed on design, colour, materials and price by operating management. A schedule of finishes should also be published and circulated to contractors.

The architectural staff should also be prepared to contribute to design ideas for shopfront and internal image and make recommendations on modules to be used. The department must be able to show cost benefits from alternative types of fitting and also to argue cases on the basis of functionalness and aesthetics. This may well apply to design details such as ashtrays, internal signing, staffroom furniture and so on.

Some of the larger retail firms retain design consultants to suggest schemes. In essence, the estates department must be able to interpret the wishes of the operators and suggest alternative design treatments.

8 MAINTENANCE

The estates department must make regular inspections of all properties owned by the company and plan and carry out a programme of maintenance. This can be budgeted for and the department is required to cost each project. A maintenance programme will be agreed by operating management and initiated both by the latter and estates.

9 OTHER STATUTORY DUTIES

Under the Offices, Shops and Railway Premises Act retailers have a duty to provide proper fire access, sanitation and staffroom accommodation. These requirements do not necessarily come under the heading of maintenance. Local health inspectors and fire officers normally point out shortcomings of this kind, but in a lamentable number of cases some retail firms do nothing until threatened with the closure of the branch. Old property is particularly prone to this justified harrassment and, if a chain owns or leases a large number of old properties, the bill for bringing the accommodation up to standard can be large. As implied above, even if budgeted for these items are often carried over from one year to the next by some companies as being non-essential, i.e. the investment does not produce any tangible profit return. This may be a mistaken view because, as conditions improve in retailing generally because of the demolition of old property and the rigour with which some local authorities put the acts into practice, a few retailers can expect that the finding and keeping of staff is not merely a matter of wage levels. The estates department should act on compulsory purchase orders and OSR notices sent to branches which must channel them to estates.

10 ASSET MANAGEMENT

One of the most important functions of the estates department is to manage the property investment of the company. This can mean several things. It can merely mean keeping the property asset at an acceptable level of maintenance so that buildings do not lose some of their value. It may mean the collection of sub-tenants' rent. To a thorough going property man it means the manipulation of the property asset to produce the best return for the company. The problem of whether to lease or to buy a property (if there is an alternative) must obviously figure in this. The sale and leaseback of freeholds can liquidate capital which may be more effectively used in other investment. The selling of property which on a historical basis has not enhanced its value compared with the average (say 8–10 per cent per annum) because of its poor or declining position, or the purchase on a speculative basis of leases or freeholds in positions which are expected to improve are other means of managing the most important capital asset which many retail firms own. There is a strong argument for retaining a property tax consultant for this type of manipulative operation. The development of certain properties (not necessarily shops) in order to enhance their value is another aspect of estates management.

The estates department is expected to organise the revaluation of the company properties, usually at 5 year intervals. Whether this information is published is quite another matter, but there are both advantages and disadvantages to an undervaluation of assets in a balance sheet.

Also under the heading of asset or estate management come the day-to-day aspects and operating routines: lease renewals as both landlord and tenant, rating and planning matters, problems relating to adjoining tenants and all the other elements that go into successful property management.

11 CONTROL OF STOCKS

Although the estates department itself may not physically control stocks of fittings, it must organise a system whereby stocks are held at convenient points so that they can be quickly transported to project sites. It may be that shopfitters can hold these stocks on the company's behalf.

12 LIAISON

The department creates a liaison between estate agents, shopfitters, contractors and so on and the company as a whole. Through estates, the development plan comes to fruition, from its inception in the development department. The check on the performance of the company's agents in this respect is the work in progress report produced by the estates department. It is important that this report is accurately and honestly framed. Expensive mistakes can be made by incompetence in property work.

5
LOCATING MARKETS

A major part of a retail firm's strategy is composed of a marketing plan of action which outlines the tactics by which the marketing function can contribute in profit terms to company goals. This chapter describes how the geographical marketing plan can be detailed in tactical or operating terms, within the framework of the organisation outlined in the preceding chapter. Succeeding chapters deal with the implementation of the plan.

Retailers have been aptly described as front line troops. Products are the ammunition in this battle and one of the central problems in retail marketing is to decide how these supplies are to be deployed. Complementary to, but rarely controlled by, the retail company are the productive and other distributive functions which, like retailing, should normally be related to and directed by a marketing plan. How these various plans interface can be crucial to the success of supplier and retailer alike.

Retail firms with a measure of vertical integration such as Boots, the Co-op and Unilever are able to control a product from its inception to its sale in the shop. An important factor in the own brand strategies of Marks & Spencer and J. Sainsbury is their insistent control over significant aspects of marketing such as price, product ingredient, pack design and so forth.

Leaving aside for the moment these notable exceptions, many retailers are charged with the successful completion of the marketing process without fully adequate tools to do this. The end product of consumer marketing is the transfer of commodities (and services) to the final buyer. This is, of course, one of the prime functions of retailing and recognition of this fact should motivate the efficient retailer to produce marketing plans which will not only complement those of the manufacturer or his agent, but will refine and improve on these plans. The retailer's plan, in its merchandising aspect, must rely on the efforts of the supplier to make his product acceptable to the customer and profitable to the re-tailer, and the retailer will attempt to maximise his profit by carrying a stock mix which will reflect these twin requirements. (Chapter 8 explains how corporate image creation can be allied to the marketing process.)

The manufacturers of consumer goods have little direct influence on the marketing plans of the retailer (we live, after all, in a competitive society), but this is fortunate only if the retailer has a clear idea of his own objectives; the results of successful retailing are, of course, fed back to the supplier who should alter his productive and distributive plans to suit current market forces. Greater control of his marketing can be achieved by the producer either by purchase of retail outlets or by selling through mail order, but the limitations on a supplier marketing his products through an independent retail chain are great. A supplier cannot, for instance, dictate the location of a multiple's branches; the decision as to whether to stock a particular brand of product in a certain branch is left to the retailer; the proportions of display space given to a supplier's products are again decided by the retailer; manufacturers' sales aids must queue with those of his competitors for space in the branches.

The manufacturer is not unaware of these problems. Cash incentives to stock certain brands are given to retailers; merchandise presentations are mounted, giving retailers the chance to see full product ranges, new lines, redesigned packs and perhaps an insight into the supplier's share of the market; special shopfittings are designed so that the retailer can give full (and occasionally over-full) exposure to the supplier's product, with suggested returns per foot run; pack jobbing and other sales promotion aids are freely offered in what has in some cases become a free-for-all where, in the battle for display space, few are the winners.

Much of this effort appears to be self-cancelling, particularly when several competing suppliers are involved. It may be that he who shouts loudest secures a disproportionate share of display, but at the end of the day it is still the retailer who must decide how he wishes to organise his available sales space. The heartening aspect is that much of the raw material upon which he can base sound trading decisions is to hand, in his own shops.

The marketing plan of the retailer is formulated in two parts. Firstly, as a merchandising plan and, secondly, as a branch location plan. These two aspects of total market planning require very different skills; one relies on the buying and selling functions of the retailer and their application to the selection and display of products in the chain's shops, while the other aspect of retail marketing involves the assessment of the geographical coverage of the chain's existing and potential branches with particular regard to their profitability. While, then, the merchandising plan is concerned with the profitability of individual products the location plan is concerned with the profitability of individual shops. The two aspects are obviously interlinked and the total marketing plan for the chain will be determined by the objectives set by the retailer.

Because several excellent books on retail merchandising have recently been published in this country, it is not the author's intention to discuss this aspect of the retail marketing plan in any depth, except where it affects the control of goods to be carried in any particular branch of a retail chain.

Buying and general stock control must have an important bearing on the profitability of each outlet and this on the chain as a whole, an importance which is emphasised in appropriate sections of this book.

Many retail companies (and this includes some of the larger multiples), carry no formal department or section to deal with that important part of retail marketing which embraces what the Americans call store location strategy. In the notional organisation chart which was shown in Fig. 2.1 this part of the company operation is carried out by the development manager and his supporting staff.

The setting up of such a department implies a rejection of the old 'intuitive' methods of selecting shop sites and framing an expansion programme. A great deal of work has been done in this country and in the United States on these particular problems and although this aspect of the marketing plan cannot yet be said to be one that can be based totally on scientific principles, much of the risk has been taken out of it. A few retail company directors have been known to attempt site acquisitions (without surveys) in their favourite English watering places but, generally speaking, if there are set objectives they are normally followed through.

PLANNING THE DEVELOPMENT AREA

BROAD METHODS

The methods by which the geographical marketing plan can be framed are to:

1 Determine the geographical areas for possible and profitable retail expansion. This will depend on the minimum acceptable support

population to show the desired return on investment and other factors as detailed in the next section.

2 Determine the sales and profit levels and market share which each potential (and existing) outlet can reasonably take as its objective by examining unit strengths and weaknesses and matching these with the standard shop profile.

3 Examine the possibilities of diversifying into other market areas by acquisition of existing businesses. This may also include diversifying into other product groups.

4 Produce a final geographical marketing plan as part of the corporate plan.

CONSTRAINTS ON DEVELOPMENT

The first part of planning a development area is to examine the constraints on extending market coverage. These are discussed below.

Physical distance This does not affect the large multiple as much as it might the smaller chain run possibly by one man, the proprietor of which must be readily able to control his shops, travelling between them by car. The bigger retail chain normally controls branches on a territory basis, each area being in the charge of a superintendent or a regional/area manager.

Lines of communication Branches, no matter whether they obtain supplies direct from the manufacturer or from a company warehouse, must be reasonably accessible by road or rail. This is particularly true of shops selling daily lines, e.g. bread and newspapers. National supermarket chains appear loath to open branches more than 100 miles from their warehouses.

Type of trade Except in the very largest cities, variety chain stores and other large space users will operate only one branch. (Current trends in other multiples such as Boots and W. H. Smith which carry a large range of commodities are towards bigger units.) The exceptions here are some supermarket chains and other food and convenience trade shops which, because of the lower support populations required, are able to open more than one branch in many towns, very often in the suburbs.

Existence of market potential Certain areas offer no scope for development because of low catchment populations, heavy competition or the smallness and undeveloped nature of shopping centres. The company concerned may already be operating a profitable branch in the area which might suffer from the competition of another branch in close proximity to it. Again, the 'image' of the company may not fit in with the socio-economic profile of the neighbourhood.

F

Finance Capital must be available to support an expansion plan, whether it be raised from profits, the public or from sale of assets. The level of interest rates, government intervention in capital projects or the general state of the economy can limit the number of outlets planned, although they may not necessarily impose limits on the geographical extent of the development area.

Availability of sites Some shopping centres are highly constricted and the number of sites appearing on the open market for sale or lease can therefore be severely limited, particularly if a number of multiple firms are attempting entry. Once on the market, the sites must necessarily be of correct size and shape; variety chains have encountered difficulty in acquiring enough land in some centres to create viable units. Rents in many of the larger and more attractive shopping centres are very high and this, again, discourages some retailers from entry, particularly if they require prime pitches.

Acquisition of businesses Taking over existing retail businesses is another method of extending a development area. Sainsbury, for instance, created the nucleus of its Midlands expansion by the purchase of Thoroughgood, a nine branch grocery firm. The merger of Boots Ltd and Timothy Whites and Taylor achieved a deepening rather than an extension of the former's development area, although the creation of a hardware chain based on the Timothy Whites operation has not damaged the Boots' market areas. Rationalisation of a development area can be one of the prime advantages of acquisition, if the shops acquired are in competition with those of the purchaser.

Legal and trade restraints Supermarket companies who intend to build branches incorporating off-licences have in the past had licences turned down by local Brewster Sessions, although unless the license is a pre-requisite for opening a supermarket this is not likely to upset development area plans. There has, in fact, been a recent softening in the legal attitude towards off-licences incorporated in supermarkets. Certain trade restrictions are sometimes enforced. For instance, newspaper publishers will hesitate to grant supplies to a new branch of a newsagent if they feel that the area is already adequately covered and that the granting of supplies might damage trade in shops in the area operated by their existing trade customers. 'Mill clearance' is required for bakery shops.

Lack of management Two limitations could exist here. Firstly, training and succession plans in the firm may be limited, with the result that an expansion plan is discouraged by the lack of branch managers to run the new shops. Secondly, an expansion plan can be stultified by a lack of professional skills at head office. Both these problems can be surmounted in time by judicious recruitment and training, as part of a corporate plan.

The constraints outlined above can impose severe limitations on the planning of a development area, but once the limits of such an area have been established, this aspect of the marketing plan can be progressed.

The next stage is to decide the towns and shopping centres in which the firm is interested in representing itself, taking note of those towns with existing branches so that optimum coverage can be achieved. J. Sainsbury Ltd works on the basis of attaining the fullest possible market coverage with the minimum number of branches. Although this chain was achieving a quite deep penetration of its markets with small (5000 ft^2 sales) outlets, the idea now is to increase the size of branches to secure more of the marginal custom within the catchment. Before producing any kind of development area list, the firm must be sure what kind of retailing operation it is setting out to be. This may already be determined by historical factors. A wise course, taking the limitations imposed by development area planning, is to base an expansion on the strategic and tactical planning described in chapter 1. In this context, a company can set future turnover and profit targets to be achieved either by more efficient use of existing outlets or by opening x number of new branches to support these objectives.

THE DEVELOPMENT AREA LISTS

It is perhaps fortuitous that an element of forward planning and profit budgeting is forced on the retailer by the workings of the property market. There are two important sources of new shop sites apart from undeveloped plots which necessitate building. One is the vacation of existing properties by other trades and the alternative is the letting of units in new shopping developments. In the latter case, a retail firm knows the approximate date on which the unit will be handed over by the developer for wet trades and subsequent fitting, and therefore the sales and profit figures resulting from the site assessment can be incorporated in forward budgets for the period after the unit is opened for trading. In the case of properties vacated by other retailers, the expanding firm has little knowledge of when particular sites are likely to come on to the market and therefore no detailed budgeting can be done for these projects. The retailer can, however, make an approach directly or through an agent to an occupier to see whether a purchase is possible. This is particularly common when a multiple wishes to extend an existing branch by taking over a flanking property; many of the variety chains attempt this rather than resiting which has the twofold difficulty of the securing of a plot large enough and disposing of the existing unit.

It is suggested that because these two sources of shop properties are so different and require different modes of approach that two development lists be created, one detailing the towns within which a firm requires representation and the other listing new shopping developments.

The town list The problem of actually framing a list of towns where sites are required is quite difficult, far more so than listing details of new shopping developments which are normally advertised in the property press or are circulated by estate agents. The retail company must decide what minimum support population it requires, the maximum level of competition, the socio-economic patterns in the population it needs to service, car parking requirements and so on as detailed in the description of the development department's functions. Again, the firm must be aware of the kind of outlet it wishes to trade in, from various points of view, including sales area, minimum acceptable sales and net profit, type of operation (e.g. self-service), 'image' and so forth. Taking the market requirements at this stage, the main points which should be covered in a survey of towns or a selected development area to give viable branches are:

1 Delineation of the catchment area.
2 Estimation of the size and socio-economic characteristics of the population within the catchment.
3 Estimation of *per capita* expenditure on the lines to be stocked in the proposed branch.
4 Estimation of the total potential expenditure on the selected commodities (by multiplying *per capita* sale per period by the catchment population or households).
5 Assessment of the expenditure going to competition within the shopping centre and/or calculation of a possible market share for the new trader in order to forecast potential branch sales.

These forecasts must take into account known future changes in the catchment population, future redevelopment and an appreciation of the possibility of changes in competition. (These factors and methods of processing them are fully detailed in the author's previous work, *Retail Site Assessment*; they are also, of course, relevant to the selection of new shopping developments.)

By taking into account the factors detailed in the previous section on the limits of development areas and the site assessment criteria outlined above, a list of suitable towns for entry can be created. It is perhaps interesting at this point to discuss some research the author carried out on the representation of a large British multiple firm within towns of varying (local authority) populations. The sample of towns refers specifically to England and Wales and excludes London boroughs and rural districts where shopping foci are much less distinctly related to the areas they service.

TABLE 5.1   Representation within various sizes of local authority by one multiple concern (1968)

Population range ('ooo)	Number of local authorities within each population band	Number of branches within each population band	Percentage representation
0–10	312	56	18
10–20	197	53	27
20–30	113	30	27
30–40	67	19	28
40–50	43	16	37
50–60	35	20	57
60–70	18	11	61
70–80	21	9	43
80–90	13	9	69
90–100	10	4	40
100–150	22	10	45
150–200	11	6	55
200–250	5	3	60
250–500	9	7	78
over 500	5	3	60

Table 5.1 shows that the multiple concern was less well represented on a percentage basis in towns of under 40,000 population (i.e. all figures below 30 per cent of total available markets). Indeed its market representation percentage only climbs over 50 per cent in towns of over 50,000. The percentage of representation falls off for a span above the 90,000 population level but this may have been due to the inability to secure sites or the presence of certain larger towns outside the multiple's current development area.

It would appear from the table that there are certain areas where the multiple was weak through poor representation, particularly in the population bands 30,000–50,000 which offer 75 towns without the multiple's presence. This gives a pointer to a competitive retailer's development area (town list).

Once it has been decided what the expansion rate for opening new branches is to be, a town list can be produced showing priorities based on population, competition, size and complement of main shopping centre. These priorities should be quantified by detailing the sales areas required as (for example) based on an average sale per square foot of £50 per year, showing the minimum sales levels and net shop areas acceptable to the company.

TABLE 5.2   Notional relationship between population,
sales and branch sales area

Catchment population ('000)	Estimated annual sales (£'000)	Sales area (ft²)
30–40	50–60	1,000–1,500
40–50	60–70	1,000–1,500
50–60	70–80	1,500
60–70	80–85	1,500–2,000
70–80	85–90	1,500–2,000
80–90	90–95	2,000
90–100	95–100	2,000
100–150	100–150	2,000–3,000
150–300	150–200	3,000–4,000
300–500	200–250	4,000–5,000

Another method of quantifying the sales and profitability which are
produced by certain environments is to match those returns in a
chain's existing shops to their support populations. Appendix IV
Tables 1 to 5 are based on actual case studies and show that, in the particular companies examined, the minimum support population required
to produce a 5 per cent net profit from a £40,000 minimum sale per
annum was 30,000.

A technique for assessing new and existing retail sites has been
developed in London by Gallup. The method is based on comparisons
with a retailer's existing branches and incorporates the following elements:

1 Internal data supplied by client.
2 Population data of catchment.
3 External factors including competition, car parking and key
   multiples.

A sample of 40 to 50 outlets in the same company is taken and about a
dozen variation factors built in; if there appear to be anomalies, up to 35
different factors are used in the calculation.

The fees for this service were quoted as £6000–7000 for a 40 to 50
shop sample and based on a 6 month assignment on fixed cost plus
variable cost. A study of 100 shops would cost approximately £10,000.
Let us look in detail at some actual development areas (see Appendix V).
This table shows the branches in the Greater London Council area of
British Home Stores, Mothercare, John Menzies and W. H. Smith, i.e.

one of the two smaller variety chains, a specialist clothing chain and two competitive multiples retailing newspapers, books, stationery and various other goods.

BRITISH HOME STORES

About 20 per cent of BHS branches (out of a total of nearly 100 branches) are located in the area under study. They are predominantly, but not entirely, to be found in shopping centres catering for a mainly working class population. Variety chains site themselves under the handicap of their size: it is difficult to assemble enough land to create the big units necessary. This may partly explain the gaps in the company's London development to date. For instance, there is no branch in Croydon or in Bromley. In the former case, BHS would require a frontage on North End which is difficult to obtain at present, while in the latter case, Bromley is rather a restricted centre as far as prime pitches go. It is interesting to note that in both of these centres Sainsbury have entered new developments associated with but off the main street. Variety chain branches will only be found in very large regional or sub-regional centres catering for catchment populations in excess of 100,000 and very often in close association with other variety stores (e.g. in Coventry and in Princes Street, Edinburgh). British Home Stores strategy of expansion is to have 120 'handpicked' stores; if a store is modernised and fails to pay, it is sold and an alternative site searched for.

MOTHERCARE

This relatively new company also has about 20 per cent of its total branches in London but has located in both the very largest and less large centres (e.g. Edmonton, Harrow and Orpington). This chain requires a minimum catchment area of 70,000 and frontages of at least 25 feet. This latter may explain some gaps in its London development, e.g. in Putney and Wembley, but the chain could obviously expand into another dozen or so medium sized London shopping centres. Mothercare with a present complement of 130 branches aims to double this figure in towns with a minimum population of 70,000. See Appendix VI.

W. H. SMITH AND JOHN MENZIES

It is interesting to compare the London coverage of these very similar multiples. Much of the Menzies development was decided in Wyman's days and little or no development has occurred since the takeover in 1959. Most of the competition between these two chains takes place in the better off north London suburbs such as Edgware, Golders Green and Wembley but there are also competitive elements in the City (Cheapside), in Belgravia (Sloane Street) and in Sutton. W. H. Smith

75

dominates the coverage of London in this particular trade, but there would appear to be openings for Menzies, on a competitive basis with Smith's, in centres like Croydon, Kingston and Romford. This particular market is, however, highly competitive, although few independent CTN (confectionery, tobacco, news) outlets wish to expand. It must be stated that unless the retailer moves in to buy a particular property, the list of towns earmarked for branches will remain merely a list, possibly divided into 'essential', 'probable' and 'possible' areas for expansion.

In the case of first class sites, retail firms may have only a few days or even hours to decide whether to take a site or not. The decision as to the purchase of leases or freeholds, then, must initially be determined by the development area list referred to above, but a sophistication can be incorporated in the bare list of towns by detailing the precise properties which the retailer would be interested in should they come on the market. Although it appears a daunting task to plan in this much detail, certain estate agents and map making companies have produced traders' key plans which show the location of each shop in a centre; prime and secondary pitches can easily be identified from such plans. Unfortunately, the plans rarely give enough detail to determine the gross area of shops, and therefore it is necessary for field work to be carried out, either by the development manager's team or by estate agents retained for this purpose.

A scale of priorities can be roughly worked out for town list sites. Those towns which are likely to offer branches with higher return on capital investment should obviously be dealt with first, provided that sites are available in these towns.

The shopping centre list   The second type of list which should be produced to aid expansion planning is that containing details of new shopping centre development. Many retailers still wish to know what other tenants have leased or reserved units in a centre not so much because of the competitive aspect, but because of the need for complementary traders and resultant associated sales. A director of J. Sainsbury Ltd, however, has said that the chain is not so interested as it was in going into developments with other traders so long as there was adequate car parking available near the centre: this has been borne out by several shopping developments in the South of England in which this multiple has located branches. It may be some time before other large multiples make this confident assertion publicly.

'For the majority of (retail) firms the planning horizon is short. The length of time involved from the active preparation of schemes to their completion is usually not more than two years and often nearer to one'.[1] This is once a firm decision has been made to enter a development.

We are talking, in effect, of a plan which will take perhaps 5 years to fulfil. The first 2 or 3 years of the plan can be framed within quite closely defined limits, but between 3 and 5 years the plan is likely to contain a large degree of flexibility. There is little merit in producing a development area plan in detail which extends over the 5 year period because of many factors which are unknown. The plan becomes really firm between one and two years before completion and this refers also to projects from the town list.

Most expansionist retailers are effectively working to a 3 year final plan. This is dictated largely by the building of new shopping development, the precise details of which are unlikely to be known until 3 years before opening. Precise knowledge is important to the retailer: he must know his eventual position in the development, the dimensions and gross area of the unit he has decided on and the rent. This knowledge allows him to incorporate the project in his forward budgeting of capital and manpower resources and because he can cost the project in profit terms and estimate sales, of his profit and sales forecasts. As the time scale shortens, budgets can be refined and updated.

EXISTING BRANCHES

Information required   As part of the corporate planning investigation of the existing structure and performance of the business (strengths and weaknesses), the retailer should survey his existing chain and the markets which his branches are operating within. The internal or *branch* information required for market planning is as follows:

1 SALES AND PROFITABILITY Branch trading accounts over a 3 year period will show trends in sales, gross and net profits and operating expenses.

2 CAPITAL INVESTMENT An up-to-date valuation of freehold properties or leases, average value of stock held and written down value of fixtures and fittings will, in total, give capital assets figure for each branch.

3 BRANCH DIMENSIONS Each branch should have, if possible, an architect's drawing showing the total area and particularly the area devoted to selling.

4 SALES AND GROSS PROFIT MIX It is important to know what sort of commodities are being sold in each branch.

The external or *market* data on existing sites required for tactical planning is as follows:

1 POPULATION Catchment area population can either be worked out by various survey methods or by referring to publications such as the *Geographia Sales Manager's Handbook.*

2 CONSUMER EXPENDITURE Individual or household expenditure for most retail trades is contained in publications such as the *Family Expenditure Survey.*

3 TYPE OF LOCATION Branches can be graded by the complement of their shopping centres, e.g. district, sub-regional or neighbourhood centres. This geographical method of grading centres can be misleading for tourist and other seasonal towns which should further be classified as 'seaside', 'inland tourist', 'commuter' and so on.

4 STRENGTH OF COMPETITION The effect of competition is difficult to assess, even by weighting their influence on the basis of multiple or independent trader designations. The author has carried out some research with various retail companies but there is no strong evidence that in some trades competition has much effect at all. This is obviously difficult to quantify because there are antithetic pressures such as the cumulative attraction to shoppers of several shops in the same trade which may extend the market area, but there is no doubt that overshopping (however that is defined) in a particular trade will reduce the market shares of the competing shops.

5 PITCH The section of a shopping centre in which a branch is located may have a significant effect on its performance. The complementary aspect of multiples together on a prime pitch generates higher pedestrian flows than in secondary sections. Some multiple retailers still depend on a head count past a potential site to aid their site assessment. The fact that the police occasionally move in (to the author's personal knowledge) does not detract from the splendid efficacy of this survey method.

Using the information Once performance and market data has been gathered for each branch the following information can be deduced:

1 RETURN ON CAPITAL INVESTMENT By computing the total assets (property, fittings, stock and possibly manager's house if company owned) and relating item to net profit a return on capital employed figure can be worked out for the past 3 years for each branch, provided that changes in the assets over the period have been taken note of.

2 SALES AND PROFIT RELATED TO BRANCH SIZE By relating sales/

profit to the net (sales) area of a branch a return per square foot or conversion factor of space devoted to trading can be gauged.

3 MARKET SHARE The total potential expenditure in each catchment area can be estimated by multiplying the catchment population by the *per capita* expenditure. By drawing the annual sales of a branch as a percentage of the annual total expenditure on commodities sold by the branch, a market share can be worked out. Sub-market shares are also available by taking the annual sales of one commodity in the branch and dividing it by the total estimated catchment expenditure on that commodity.

4 OTHER DATA This information (type of location, pitch, competition) is less relateable to branch performance although with a large enough sample of branches some consistencies are likely to be thrown up. For instance, the size of a shopping centre is quite often related to the size of its support population and this, in turn, must have an effect on branch sales and thus profitability.

The manager of a non-competing multiple branch may be prepared to disclose his branch sales to another retailer nearby. This information can be matched up with the retailer's own branch performance, after making allowances for different sales levels in different trades. Unfortunately, average sales in some trades are relatively meaningless to other retailers (for instance a baker's shop taking £800 per week would be regarded in the baking trade as being a volume unit, this sales level being about twice the average).

One of the advantages accruing to market researchers in the multiple retail trade is the large amount of comparative data that can be mined from a chain's results and this information, if properly collated and used, is the basis for a strategic appraisal of a multiple's marketing policies. A retail firm cannot fairly plan its future without the sort of information detailed above and set out on a comparative basis. An obvious idea is to plot existing (and proposed) branches on a development area map. This will show areas where infilling is required and this information should aid the compilation of a town list for development.

The survey will in addition have thrown up a considerable amount of data on the chain's strengths and weaknesses. For instance, it may be that a large number of shops are returning sales and profit figures below the average. This may be due to several factors: unit sizes smaller than required, incorrect stock mix, poor level of branch management, bad sites, incorrect or old fashioned in-store layouts and fittings and so on. Weaknesses of this kind and some pointers towards their correction are discussed in chapter 7. The use of market research in existing branches can produce useful data and the reader's attention is drawn to the questionnaire in Appendix VII.

Retail management must know what the minimum acceptable sales and net returns are for the company and also the minimum return on capital invested. A decision may be made, after the investigation described above, that certain branches are incapable of further development and that they should be closed. It depends on the trade, but the criteria could be £1000 sales per week and a net profit (without head office charges being taken into account) of 5 per cent, with a minimum return on capital of 15 per cent. The company can then make up a list of branch disposals and put them on the market through the estates department.

Naturally, a full investigation into the capabilities of these shops should be mounted before they are closed.

INVESTMENT AND RATIONALISATION

We now discuss what may be termed sub-tactical planning for the market. The multiple retailer will already have a stock of shops, some of which come up to the profit criteria laid down in the marketing plan and others which do not and cannot be improved to bring them up to standard.

The retail firm must obviously concentrate its efforts on those outlets which are viable and can be made more so by judicious investment.

Modernisation Shops are normally refitted towards the end of the average 10 year life of shopfittings. It is possible that a refit may come before this time in order to combat local competition or for experimental purposes. A refit need not be total and 'semi-refit' is a term commonly used in retailing, sometimes to describe the introduction of a new shop-front or counters. Only branches which are likely to benefit from modernisation should be so treated and they, of course, would be expected as minimum requirements not only to be capable of repaying the annual depreciation charge on the new fittings but also producing extra profit over and above this to service the capital investment.

Resites It sometimes occurs that a branch has to resite because of changes in the shopping environment, e.g. the move of a key multiple or a new traffic management scheme. Occasionally, an offer is received from another trader and, if acceptable, the branch must be resited if it is felt worthwhile staying in that particular centre. Leases fall due, compulsory purchase orders are tendered and so on. Very often, however, a resite occurs because the branch is trading above the capacity it was designed for and there is no possibility of extending backwards or sideways to secure more sales area. When a resite occurs it normally means that trade has to be transferred to a new and completely fitted out shop. Resites should be looked at very carefully as they sometimes tend to

produce a lesser return than do extended branches. By replacing a
£1000 per week shop by one taking £1500 means, in effect, the opening
of a new branch taking only £500, with all the extra cost of new fittings,
restocking and so forth. Sometimes the old fittings in the discarded
branch can be utilised elsewhere. If they cannot, and they have not been
completely written off, their charges should fall on the resited branch. A
development area list (see Appendix VI) should contain notes on planned resites. As explained above, some resites cannot be budgeted for.

Extensions It is often possible to extend branches once they have
become too small for their sales level. 'Most of our stores are single-
storey affairs so we can either build up or extend backwards' says
Marcus Sieff, joint managing director, of Marks & Spencer, explaining
a main thread in this multiple's expansion strategy. Occasionally this is
possible by reorganising the stock accommodation and pushing the sales
area backwards to take up the area released, but it often means the purchase of flanking traders' units. This can be planned and budgeted for
by observing the sales trends in a particular branch. This is normally a
better method of gaining extra sales space than by resiting, particularly
if the pitch the branch occupies is prime. A resite, even to larger
premises, can sometimes lose potential market share because of a transfer
to a less busy section of a shopping centre. There is always the compensation of lower rent and rates, however, but this is not an argument
which figures large in most multiple retailers' minds. If there is no possibility of an extension (because flanking traders have categorically
refused to sell) the only alternative, if the firm wishes to continue
trading in the town, is to search for an alternative site.

Acquisition of existing businesses By buying existing shops owned by
competing or even non-competing traders, a retail company can not only
extend its development area but carry out plans for rationalising the
spread of shops. Birrel, the confectioner and tobacconist chain, have
been carrying this out after their purchase of McColl; and so have Boots
with Timothy Whites and Tesco with Victor Value. Many firms which
have produced corporate plans specifically name the companies which
they hope to take over, either purely for investment purposes or in order
to rationalise their development area coverage, help their central buying
power, cream off executives and so on. (See page 37 for a discussion on
mergers as such.) If a complete large company is to be taken over, it is
likely that a budget can be framed for it sometime in advance of the
approach. The purchase of small companies or single shops cannot be
pre-planned.

It is sometimes possible, although not always successful, to diversify
into a completely different market by purchase of existing businesses.

REVENUE BUDGETING

SALES

An essential part of retail market planning is the forecasting of sales in branches over the whole company. This should be dealt with in the retail division or department of a company because the raw statistical material and other supporting information from company records is more readily available there than through, say, the financial division or accounting department. It is suggested that the budgets could be framed by the development manager and his staff. This would take some of the workload off the operating management and, as can be seen in chapter 4, a large development department should contain sufficient skills to carry out this task (although this is not specifically suggested). The actual physical handling of the data and its formalisation in account or budget form would, of course, be left to the accountants with their particular skills in data presentation.

Before branch sales statistics can be used in any meaningful form they must be examined for any exceptional or non-recurring events which may have taken place and been reflected in sales. The refitting of a shop, change in management, introduction of local traffic management schemes and a host of other factors may create sales levels which are out of the ordinary. The branch manager's weekly report should list any local exceptions which might contribute to a marked increase or decrease in sales.

Before sales statistics can be processed by the development department, they must also be comparable in the sense that each week during, say, a year's trading period can be matched with a similar week in the previous period to gauge the trend. This is why most retail firms now use four 13-week trading periods rather than 12 monthly periods to obviate the problem of differing month lengths and composition.

The simplest means of monitoring sales for budget and comparison purposes is to use the moving annual total (MAT) method by which over a year's trading each month's sales are added and the corresponding month during the previous year subtracted. The advantage of the MAT is that it smooths seasonal trends and shows the upward or downward changes in sales. The MAT is seen to best advantage on a graph which may also contain a budgeted increase line (say 6 per cent) with which the MAT line can be compared. A so-called 'Z-chart' can also be constructed, showing actual sales, cumulative sales and MAT (see Fig. 5.1). The construction of such a graph requires no statistical knowledge at all; there are other rather more sophisticated methods of graphically representing sales and the author would refer to the Bibliography for works dealing with these.

Sales trends are affected, as has been hinted, by factors other than

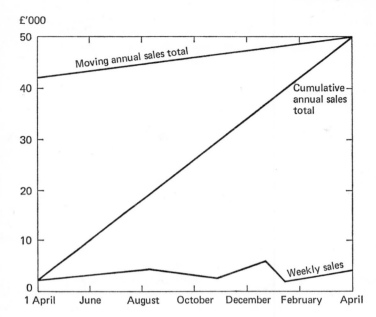

Fig. 5.1   A 'Z' chart for retail branch sales monitoring.

internal which may have resulted, company wide, from sales promotion schemes, new lines, price adjustments and so on. The external environment in the rather nebulous shape of market forces and in the more concrete form of government action must obviously affect sales within a retail company. As explained previously, one of the trends of the development department can and should be the monitoring of reports from government, business and press sources.

Summarising, the forecast sales of a company are primarily dependent on the trend unearthed by study of the MAT. The more historical sales data available, the more accurate should be the projection. Greater accuracy in budgeting for a complete retail company is also possible the greater the number of branches operated. A sales forecast should be built up by examining the trend in each branch separately and adding the individual budgets together, taking into account the two types of external factor which may influence budgets. Local factors will naturally affect individual branches while national factors will affect the company's budget as a whole. Events which have occurred in the past, if significant, should be reflected in past sales and these events should be taken into account when framing budgets. All known factors which are to take place in the future must be carefully examined for their effect on sales.

83

This is the most difficult part of forecasting and requires a great deal of skill to carry out successfully. How successful forecasting is can be gauged by examining the sales data as they come in from the branches and matching them against budgets.

EXPENSES AND PROFIT

Once sales forecasts have been estimated and agreed, the company is in a position to frame its buying policy for the next period. This is done by breaking budgeted sales down into commodity groups, the forecast sales mix showing the amount of each product the firm must buy to attain the projected sales level. The total notional gross profit can then be calculated and used as part of the company budget. This should be handled by the merchandising department, in tandem with the accountants.

It follows from this point that once expenses have been budgeted for (and again historical date must be used, refined by knowledge of price or volume increases), a trading and profit and loss budget for the company can be framed and a net profit forecast worked out. This is strictly an accounting function although, as with all budgets, the operating managers must agree the figures before they are published.

Budgeting for retail firms is dealt with much more fully in other works on the subject and this rather skimped discussion is not meant to devalue its great importance, but it is not the intention of this book to deal in detail with this area of retail operation.

FINAL GEOGRAPHICAL MARKETING PLAN

We are now in a position to produce the section of the marketing plan which embraces the branch location strategy and the investigation can be quantified in budget terms.

Let us assume that a retail company made sales through its branches in 1971 of £30 millions and was budgeting for a 10 per cent increase in sales from more efficient market penetration in existing shops. The company planned to open 12 new outlets between 1972 and 1974, to modernise 14 branches by end 1973 and close 10 uneconomic branches by end 1972.

Table 5.3 shows how a shopping centre development list can be produced in budget form. Estimated profit/loss forecasts may also be incorporated. The 'town list' can be dealt with in similar fashion.

Table 5.4 shows the forecast increase in sales from the planned modernisation programme (branches listed by their code number).

We now have a simple set of figures from which a sales budget for 1972 can be worked out. If sales increase is projected by 10 per cent,

Plate 1   *Mothercare—Store Exterior (Rodøvre, Denmark).*   (Courtesy: Mothercare)

Plate 2 Mothercare—Own Brand Pack.   (*Courtesy: Mothercare*)

TABLE 5.3 Budgeted sales increases from contracted sites in certain shopping centres, 1972–74

Town/shopping centre	Completion for trading	Budgeted sales at 1971 prices (£)
Town 1 shopping centre a	1972	100,000
Town 2 shopping centre b	1972	150,000
Town 3 shopping centre c	1972	120,000
Town 4 shopping centre d	1972	200,000
Budgeted sales from new shops, 1972:		570,000
Town 5 shopping centre e	1973	300,000
Town 6 shopping centre f	1973	250,000
Budgeted sales from new shops, 1973:		550,000
Town 7 shopping centre g	1974	70,000
Town 8 shopping centre h	1974	100,000
Town 9 shopping centre j	1974	100,000
Town 10 shopping centre k	1974	80,000
Town 11 shopping centre l	1974	200,000
Town 12 shopping centre m	1974	60,000
Budgeted sales from new shops, 1974:		610,000

TABLE 5.4 Budgeted sales increases from modernisation 1972–73

Branch to be refitted	Year of completion of refit	Budgeted sales increase at 1971 prices (first year) (£)
Branch 37	1972	12,000
Branch 142	1972	8,000
Branch 6	1972	50,000
Branch 236	1972	27,000
Branch 190	1972	16,000
Branch 44	1972	10,000
Budgeted sales increase from refits, 1972		123,000
Branch 200	1973	20,000
Branch 97	1973	70,000
Branch 22	1973	15,000
Branch 79	1973	15,000
Branch 2	1973	8,000
Branch 56	1973	100,000
Branch 47	1973	17,000
Branch 111	1973	35,000
Budgeted sales increase from refits, 1973		280,000

G

sales without the uplift from investment in existing and new branches will be £33 millions. By adding in the forecasts for new and refitted shops due to come on stream in 1972, the budgeted sales are then £33,693,000.

But it is also planned to close 10 small uneconomic branches in 1971–72 with a combined sale of £327,000. The budgeted sales figure for 1972 would then be £33,366,000. It is assumed, however, that the sales cut off by such a programme of closures are loss making. Let us say that the disposed of shops were losing £18,000 per annum between them and that the modernised shops in 1972 are planned to contribute profit increases of £10,000. We then have a net increase in profits of £28,000 against which must be set the loss making or break-even positions of the newly acquired branches.

It is obviously difficult to make an accurate budget forecast for shops when the exact date of their increased or new profitability is unknown.

SOURCES AND REFERENCES

1 *Productivity and Capital Expenditure in Retailing.* K. D. George and P. V. Hills. C.U.P., 1968.

6
PLANNING BRANCHES

This chapter deals with the implementation of the development area plans, and explains the mechanisms whereby new sites are selected and branches planned up to handover to operational management. Much of the description is relevant to resited, extended and modernised branches as well as the purchase of existing similar businesses, but the special criteria used to assess existing branch performance and investment requirements are described more fully in chapter 7.

FLOW OF INFORMATION

We have seen how the vital guides to expansion, the development area lists, are determined. The lists are not only a check for the shop development and operating sections to work by, but should be circulated to those estate agents which deal with retail outlets on a national or regional basis.

Although the creation of these lists may initially and primarily be done through desk research, it is essential that they be kept up to date. This can be done by circulating regional lists to area managers or superintendents, who are then charged with sending up-to-date information to the development department. Within some retail firms, a measure of responsibility is put on the branch manager himself to report on competition changes and on local redevelopment. (In variety chain stores, assistant managers are sent out to the local branches of their competitors to check on new lines, display footages for certain best selling products, colour ranges and so on.) One well known and very successful supermarket company encourages its branch managers to send local news cuttings on new shopping developments and plans of their own shopping centres showing competing stores, to head office where they are carefully filed for reference. A consistently high quality of branch manager is required for this and he is expected to carry out much of this work in his spare time.

It is useful to stress to those managers charged with doing this sort of work, whether they be branch managers or company/area retail managers, that the results can be beneficial to the local manager if and only if head office acts on reliable information to counter competition, improve branch location or, as long as the location falls within the lists that head office has approved, to set up entirely new outlets. Such a feedback of information can be built into management guides (if management by objectives is being operated in a company) or by some other type of regular reporting system.

Such a system does not, of course, absolve the development manager and his staff from extracting information from the Multiple Shops' Federation reports, the estates and national press and from simple observation as head office retail staff move around the country. At head office level, useful contacts can be set up by various methods with development and estates sections in other retail firms: the sharing of experience which results can often either compound or counter the enthusiasm of an estate agent letting, say, a new shopping development.

In summary, then, all concerned with retailing at whatever level should be encouraged to report on changes occurring within the chain's development area so that the fullest information is available to operational and development management.

SPECIFICATION FOR NEW BRANCHES

The previous section may have appeared to minimise the help which the estate agent can give to the retailer—which can be considerable—but the retailer alone knows what his requirements are and nowhere is this more true than with the specifications for many potential branches. The development department, in consultation with general retail management will decide the approximate requirements for new sites. The development manager should have a particularly important say in this, in the author's view, because his department has collated and interpreted the data flowing from existing branches; this function cannot be carried out adequately by operating management because of the deep involvements in the actual running of the shops. This advice is then passed on to the estates department who are charged with circulating the specifications to the agents selected for their coverage.

The main points of such a brief apart from the actual town or shopping centre are:

1 Maximum rent for a leasehold or maximum cost (preferably rentalised) for a freehold property.
2 Unit dimensions.
3 Pitch.

We now discuss these points more fully.

I RENT

Rent or property price is theoretically determined by balancing the value set on the property by the seller and the buyer respectively, i.e. by supply and demand. Certain traders are prepared to pay high prices for the pitch and unit dimensions most suited to their requirements; from the retailer's point of view the acceptability of a particular rent must, in the last resort, be determined by his ability to pay it. This can fairly easily be worked out by constructing an operational budget which must, of course, be based on a sales estimate. Total occupancy costs include rent and rates which may be set at a maximum of, say, 10 per cent of estimated sales depending on the other components of the running costs, e.g. wages, annual depreciation or head offices charges. The retailer can gauge these costs by reference to the performances of similar existing branches. If a freehold property is to be purchased, a sale and leaseback costing will also determine the market rent, but the interest charged depends to some extent on the strength of the retailer's covenant.

Rents offered can sometimes be reduced by negotiation, but location has the greatest bearing on the size of the rent. In determining the rack rent (i.e. the rent of a site improved with buildings) there are certain factual and legal considerations which must be taken into account.

Factual considerations

1 POPULATION OF TOWN OR CATCHMENT AREA In normal circumstances, the larger the population serviced by a shopping centre, the higher will be the rental values.

2 TYPE OF CENTRE The place of the shopping centre within the so-called shopping hierarchy, e.g. regional or suburban centres will be in direct proportion to rentals.

3 POSITION OF SHOP IN CENTRE The rental values in those parts of the shopping centre favoured by certain multiples are much greater than at the extremities of the area.

89

4 SIDE OF STREET One side of a shopping street is invariably more popular than another because of pedestrian flows, presence of magnets, position of sun and so on.

5 PROXIMITY OF KEY TRADERS The arrival of a key trader such as Marks and Spencer in an indifferent pitch can transform values overnight.

6 PEDESTRIAN TRAFFIC FLOWS Pedestrian crossings, bus stops, crush barriers and other physical and psychological barriers to easy foot traffic can affect flows.

7 VEHICULAR TRAFFIC FLOWS Traffic management schemes which create faster denser traffic flows, such as one way streets, are unpopular with traders and this tends to depress rental values. Experimental schemes for traffic free streets as in Norwich's London Street tend to reverse this effect.

8 PARKING FACILITIES The rental value of shopping positions is enhanced by the provision of nearby parking. In Guildford the J. Sainsbury supermarket is directly accessible by lift to a multistorey car park and this proximity of supermarket to car parking is an increasingly common occurrence.

9 FRONTAGE AND DEPTH Certain multiples are prepared to pay high prices to secure the frontage and depth of unit most suited to their trading needs.

10 AREA A rectangular area is worth more in rental terms than an irregularly shaped unit with the same foot frontage.

11 OTHER ACCOMMODATION Some trades, particularly supermarkets, require as much storage as living area. Living accommodation above the shop may be essential.

12 STATE OF REPAIRS The effect on value of a poor state of repair generally varies inversely with the importance of the shopping centre.

Legal considerations

1 PREMIUM This is a capital payment in lieu of whole or part of the rent of a leasehold property and is normally rentalised and added to the actual rent to obtain a true rack rent.

2 LENGTH OF LEASE A trader proposing to carry out costly capital improvements requires a long lease to write off the investment.

3 RENT REVIEW CLAUSES The effect of such a clause in the lease is to uplift the rent after a stated number of years (7, 14 and 21 being common periods) to the rental value at that time due to inflated

costs. The absence of rent review clauses improves the value of the lease to the retailer.

4 REPAIRING OBLIGATIONS The lease may contain onerous obligations which, for a property in poor repair, could make the shop worthless.

5 INSURANCE PROVISIONS A lease which determines who pays the insurance premiums will affect the rent to a small extent.

6 RIGHTS The right of the tenant to assign, sublet, change the use of or modify the property can sometimes be constricting to the potential tenant.

7 SERVICE CHARGES These are sometimes specified in leases and are the annual amount to be charged by the landlord for providing services, if any, such as heating, lighting, cleaning of yards, porterage and so on. Service charges are becoming more important as the number of covered shopping centres grows, with air conditioned malls and salaried management.

Some traders prefer to buy freeholds due to substantial rises in property values, but these increases are not necessarily occurring today over the country as a whole. Such a policy should be more selective in present market conditions. It should be remembered that the return on capital employed in the business should exceed that returned from investment in property, but one of the reasons for freehold purchase is, of course, the greater security of tenure that this can afford. It is probable that capital could even on a long term basis be much more profitably employed in stockholding than in bricks and mortar.

Quinquennial revaluations of property investment keep a check on the change in the property complement of the total asset holding of the firm and also reveal the true return on capital.

2 UNIT DIMENSIONS

The gross area of a site must be large enough to allow sufficient stock-room and other service space to be incorporated in the new shop, having regard to the requirements of the trade, leaving a net area of floor space large enough to contain sales up to the ultimate forecast given by the development department. It is likely, particularly in prime pitches in large town centres, that the total area will be contained on more than one floor, but if the trader has any objection to this, the agent should be notified.

The net frontage should be wide enough to allow a standard shop-front to be inserted and show passers-by what the shop contains. The unit may incorporate different widths at various points in its depth, but the shell should be wide enough to contain any free standing fittings the retailer may wish to use, allowing sufficient aisle spaces (minimum of 5 feet in any self-selection operation). Ideally the unit should be squared off (rectangular). Standard unit frontages range from 15 to 20 feet, but larger multiples would normally take at least two units to secure the frontage and gross area they require. In many new developments today, a few multiples are regarded as major space users and have units tailor-made for them on the understanding that they lease the unit allocated to them. This applied particularly to supermarkets and departmental stores which are also looked upon as magnets but quite recently other traders, carrying very wide ranges, have also been classed as major space users. The term 'medium space user' is also now in vogue. This would apply to those retailers who wish to take more space than that offered by the standard unit in a development.

The built depth in a new unit should allow sufficient ground floor trading because this is the area where volume sales are achievable. When an older property is taken over the shop depth may have to be increased, taking over some of the balance of the total or built depth. This is not always possible without large scale reconstruction because of the pos-sibility of load bearing wall between the shop and the 'back shop'. The depth of a shop should in all cases be sufficient to contain certain free standing units if self-service or self-selection style of operation is envisaged.

The retailer should also stipulate, if possible, the position and width of stairways, particularly those used for taking customers from floor to floor. Minimum and maximum head room are also important because of the possible expenditure on false ceilings and the possibility of head-rooms too low for comfortable shopper circulation.

It is sometimes necessary, particularly in suburban locations, for manager's accommodation to be available above the shop. In this type of location the rent chargeable to a flat or other dwelling incorporated in the building is quite low because it does not take up valuable selling or stock space. In a prime position in a town centre this space would be utilised by the retailer for selling, stock or sublet to another user, for example as offices.

3 PITCH

Estate agents grade sections of shopping centres as 'prime multiple', 'multiple', 'secondary' and so on. The retailer must have a reasonable idea of the type of pitch that he requires. Most multiple companies are loath to enter secondary positions because of their lack of comple-mentary multiple traders. Some multiples retain and update lists of shopping streets, even down to street numbers, which they would be interested in representing themselves in. This type of information makes the agent's job much easier. Traders' key plans are useful tools for pin-pointing pitches.

Type of pitch is reflected in the rental charged as stated above. It is normally unwise for a retailer without a strong identity (and all the things that contribute to it) to gamble on a prime pitch at a high rent.

SITE ASSESSMENT REPORT

Once information on a particular site has come in from the agent and it appears to satisfy the criteria laid down for new sites, the site assessor makes an on-the-spot survey to check pitch, competition, pedestrian flows and other factors, and then, if possible, gathers information for a sales estimate. (See Appendix VIII.) The agent involved should be informed of the company's interest as soon as the detail is received by the development manager.

Once a future sales estimate has been finalised, a proposed stock mix and estimated operating costs can be worked out, along with return on capital, etc.

EXAMPLES

TABLE 6.1   Estimated sales per department in proposed supermarket

Department	Estimated sales contribution (%)	Estimated annual sales (£)
Grocery and provisions	60	60,000
Fresh meat	20	20,000
Produce	10	10,000
Bakery/confectionery	5	5,000
Non-foods	5	5,000
Totals	100	100,000

If we assume, for simplicity, that the average margin on all lines is 18 per cent, the annual gross profit at this turnover level would be £18,000. An operating budget would look something like the following.

TABLE 6.2   Budgeted operating costs

Gross profit		£18,000
Less Wages (6%)	£6,000	
Rent and rates ($3\frac{1}{2}$%)	3,500	
Other expenses (3%)	3,000	
Total operating costs		12,500
Net profit		£5,500 ($5\frac{1}{2}$%)

If we further assume that estimated fitting-out costs on this leased supermarket were £8500, taking standard costs per square foot, and that stock is turned on average once every 3 weeks, the total capital investiture is approximately £13,500. The return on capital can be expressed as:

$$\pounds\frac{5,500}{13,500} \times \frac{100}{1} = 40\cdot7 \text{ per cent}$$

It is unlikely in larger new shops that the estimated ceiling turnover will be achieved for several months or years, and therefore at least two estimates of sales, stock mix and so on are produced, one interim and the other ultimate.

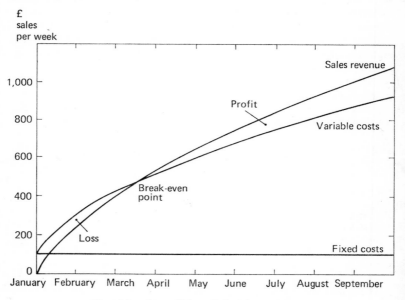

Fig. 6.1   A retail branch break-even chart.

Some firms produce several project profiles, covering the first, second, third and fifth years of operation. It is useful to construct break-even charts to illustrate this phasing (see Fig. 6.1). In the author's experience, small food shops, provided that they are correctly sited and managed, find little difficulty in achieving their ultimate sales levels within 12–18 months of opening. Tesco supermarkets are expected to make profits after the first month, while British Home Store branches take 2 years. According to research by George and Hills 'the profitability of projects was found to be very sensitive to different levels of turnover, especially when rent forms an important part of total turn-over'.[1] A very few retail firms use cash flow calculations to appraise projects. An example of this technique is given in Appendix Xa.

REPORT PRESENTATION

The report should then be discussed between the operating managers and the development staff and, if the site is accepted, the estates manager should then be asked to pass on the decision to the agent involved subject to survey and contract. Some agents are often interested in the reasons for rejecting what they consider to be a first class site (although again in the author's experience over 90 per cent of agents' details are for properties unacceptable, for various reasons, to their prospective clients); this is done so that the agents are in a position to refine their researches for their client.

Once the project has been accepted in principle, the development budget must be checked to see that the estimated capital expenditure is possible during the year in which the project will come on stream. Furthermore, the estimated sales and profit should be added in to that particular year's revenue budget and to those for succeeding years.

SURVEY, CONTRACT AND PLANNING APPLICATION

The estates manager, after agreement in principle to take the property, should have the site surveyed professionally either by his own staff or by surveyors retained for this purpose. This will not only pinpoint any structural problems but will give some idea of rebuilding costs, if appropriate. This information should be fed back to the development department so that ROCE estimates can be further refined if necessary. The survey will also help the estates department to draw up an architect's plan of the building for planning and layout purposes, if an up-to-date drawing does not exist. Estates should furnish the development manager with such a plan so that the shop planner can design the new branch layout.

The estates department should send a copy of the draft contract as soon as possible to the company legal department or solicitors so that any contentious clauses can be examined by all concerned, including operating management and appropriate advice given. After agreement, contracts can then be exchanged.

It may be that the company fits out its branches with standard ser-vices whose specifications have been agreed beforehand by operating management. It is, however, important that the type of heating, lighting, ventilation and floor covering should be known and approved by management because of the costs of running and maintenance to be charged against the branch.

Plans of the property should be submitted to the local planning authority, again after the agreement of operating management. The next stage is the design and planning of the branch layout which is discussed in the next section.

PLANNING BRANCH LAYOUTS

One of the crucial problems facing retailers is how to maximise the return from the space in branches. When we consider that each square foot of gross space can cost £10 or more per year to operate, the economics of efficient shop organisation become obvious. The revenue required to cover this outlay must be maximised by a shop layout which reduces to a minimum the amount of inactive space in the branch while giving the operator the fullest possible exposure to his products. This must be achieved without causing stock to become insecure, but allowing the customer to handle and select the goods on sale in the least effort-making way.

A large amount of theory surrounds the technique of shop design and layout and, as some retailers are not very good at reading plans, the practical application of a particular design occasionally produces a startling lack of resemblance to the original drawing. It is therefore vital that the shop planner should talk the same language as the operating managers. It is essential, for instance, to have an agreed catalogue of fittings, each unit properly designated by a code number so that the operating managers know exactly what fittings are to go into a new branch and, moreover, to be able to visualise the function of the fitting once it is merchandised. Visualisation can be aided either by models or by sketches. If wall fittings are used to any large extent, a standard treatment of corners should be agreed between the estates department and operating management. The theoretical and practical aspects of shop layout are now discussed under two main headings: design and organisation.

I DESIGN

General layout A standard form of plan should be produced for discussion by the shop planner. This should be to scale (say I cm to I metre) and show the entire area leased or owned for retail purposes. The plan should show the following:

> I SHOPFRONT Plan view should indicate the position and number of doors and windows with dimensions, and a front elevation

showing the fascial treatment, door rails, letter box position and all other relevant details.

2 MAIN SALES AREAS In plan, the position of stairs, pillars, exits, lighting, heating and electrical points along with the dimensions and location of all department fittings and the approximate positions of free standing fittings should be given. A side elevation should show stair and pillar positions and ceiling treatment (if appropriate), ceiling height and any changes in floor levels.

3 ANCILLARY AREAS Positions of stockroom, staffroom, offices and toilets should be shown in plan and elevations, with a full stockroom fitting layout superimposed.

Having made these rather obvious comments, let us discuss their implications in more detail.

It is useful to read the plans with reference to the schedule of materials and finishes produced by the estates department as well as the catalogue of fittings. This will be particularly important on checking branch image and any change from standard materials used should be indicated on the plan. The use of a doormat at the entrance will preclude the placing of free standing fittings very close to the doors. The doors should have free space behind them, depending on the size of the branch, at least large enough to allow comfortable circulation of customers entering, exiting and pausing at the entrance. Much has already been written on shop layout, but the basic theoretical and practical usages which should be followed in designing a layout are as follows.

Accessibility Assuming a self-service or self-selection style of operation, the goods on display should be easily handled by customers (paraphrasing some retail prophet or other: 'If the goods can't be stolen, they won't be sold') and the layout of the shop should bring customers into visual and physical contact with every item for sale. This means that free standing fittings should not be so high that customers sight lines are obscured into and across the shop. A maximum height of 5 feet is quite adequate for gondola displays. The uninterrupted view that customers gain in a Marks & Spencer branch is an ideal example of how fittings can be designed to allow an obstruction-free view.

Other physical and psychological obstructions which may impede accessibility are aisles which are too narrow, suppliers' display stands, fixtures across customer flow and congested space at service counters and checkouts. Pillars, staircases, window beds and backs may also hamper accessibility. The latter problems are often met with when old property is purchased and, although a certain amount of revamping in the form of shopfitting can take place, the position of supporting pillars and staircases cannot normally be altered without extensive re-building and use of RSJs. Another point is that customers very often wish to gauge the size of a shop before entering so as to give them an idea whether the shop carried a full range of departments, and it may there-fore be important for them to be able to see the back of the shop without going through the entrance doors.

The problem of accessibility in all its forms has an important lesson for the retailer. The more obstruction-free the shop, the greater the degree of security he can count on. A shop which is not blocked off by obstructions will give greater freedom to the customer to browse and purchase, but will hamper the efforts of the shoplifter. Pilferage rates in well laid out stores should as a result be lower. One could also suggest that higher productivity is possible in that assistance is more likely to be on hand to make a sale in this situation where coverage is easier.

Customer flow   A good store layout should have as one of its objectives the controlling of customer flow round the store. This does not mean forcing customers round, since the strategic placing of fittings and merchandise to block natural flows has been proved in the past to be counter-productive. Flows should be regulated, however, because too many alternative directions of movement can be confusing to customers. Fittings, particularly free standing types, should be arranged so that customers will move voluntarily in the desired direction. This can be aided by the use of store guides and commodity signs and the strategic positioning of high demand merchandise as 'magnets'. All these sug-gestions contain their own pitfalls, however, if progressed to their ulti-mate conclusion and we further discuss some of them under the next major heading 'organisation'.

Stockroom   The prime functions of a stockroom can be detailed as follows:

1 To hold buffer stocks of a few items which are infrequently delivered.
2 Unwrapping deliveries.
3 Checking deliveries against invoice.
4 Price marking.

Stockrooms, on the other hand, should not be used to hold extra stocks to take advantage of better terms or as a hedge against possible shortage of certain lines. In a self-service or self-selection style of operation, the bulk of goods in the shop should, of course, be on display. There are inherent dangers in allowing too large a stock area: the bigger the stockroom and its stockholding, the less close the supervision is likely to be and therefore the greater the security risk. A large stockroom tends to become untidy, which may lead to loss, damage or deterioration. Double handling of stock, from goods reception into stockroom and thence to selling area increases costs.

Stockrooms become less necessary if the branch is either supplied by a central warehouse or direct from the supplier. A stockroom, then, if it is necessary must be designed for the budgeted stockholding of the branch, and should also conform in its layout to the principles of accessibility and customer flow.

2 ORGANISATION

Location of departments   Broadly speaking, the higher the price of an object the longer the time necessary for the customer to make the buying decision. Higher price items should therefore be located towards the rear of the shop to avoid obstruction to customer flow. In addition, personal service departments hold up customer flow and should therefore be positioned to avoid restriction.

Merchandise grouping   There are three broad types of merchandise as defined by customer intention to buy. They are *demand* items which the customer intends to purchase and which are probably on her shopping list, if she has one; *reminder* items which she would have intended to purchase but which she has overlooked; and *impulse* items which she had not intended to purchase at all, but which can be made appealing by skilful presentation.

Building on these loose definitions, demand items can be used to boost customer flows within the shop while impulse and reminder lines can be presented alongside. This does not mean that the layout of merchandise should be based on the retailer's conception of what the customer requires. Grouping should conform to the customer's convenience and understanding of the layout should be aided by signs which are simply printed in clear type with unambiguous wording. Merchandise of similar type should be grouped together in a store; the larger the store the more important this grouping is. Groupings should be logical from the customer's point of view and not grouped for administrative convenience.

Cash points   A full self-service layout is normally served by banks of checkouts, but a self-selection or part self-service operation must contain separate cash registers. These registers may be allocated to cash-and-wrap points which would cover several departments or they may be placed on counters at which service is offered. Customers must be encouraged to pay where they wish at a cash/wrap point. These points should be dispersed to match transactions from various departments. Because cash/wrap is often centrally placed, supervision is quite easy.

Space allocation It is initially assumed that any site bought will contain sales up to the level envisaged in the site investigation and will allow for any known increase in sales volume. Supermarkets plan ahead by buying sites which will not be used to capacity for 2 or more years and leave space at the front of the store for extra checkouts. If the average sale per square foot per annum for a chain is, say, £50 and the ultimate sales estimate is £300,000 p.a., the unit would have to contain a net (sales) area of 6000 ft².

The breaking down of a total sales estimate into departmental or category sales (see Table 6.1) gives some indication of the space required for each department. If, as in a supermarket, sections are located on opposite sides of a gangway it is not helpful to work on the basis of an annual department sale per square foot; this can only be done meaningfully in an area of the store which is self-contained and which carries only one category of goods. There are several methods of measuring performance in retail outlets and deciding what display proportions to allocate to various commodity categories.

In variety chain stores the measurement is in sales per foot of display. As the bulk of display in variety stores is on island counters (with sides and ends amounting in total to about 50 feet) it is fairly easy to measure performance and allocate displays. For instance, if a full counter displaying men's trousers was taking £500 per week the sale per foot run per week would be £10.

If, for argument's sake, the average sale per foot run for the chain in this commodity was £20, then the idea would be to cut trouser displays by half and use the rest of the counter for some other (sympathetic) line which appeared to be underdisplayed elsewhere in the store, again taking the chain's average returns into account.

Other methods of measuring sales performance which are used in self-service or self-selection outlets include measuring shelf footages on walls and free standing units, and dividing sales by the total display footage allocated to a particular category; the amount of vertical and horizontal wall space may also be measured to give a figure for wall square feet, for example a 40 foot run of stationery shelving taken to 6 feet above floor level would give a square footage of 240 which can then be divided into sales, and free standing units can be incorporated in this latter measurement without too much difficulty.

A further refinement of this type of performance assessment, as used for working out displays for new shops, is to calculate the gross profit return per module of display. As the intention is to utilise the space available in new shops as profitably as possible, it is important to take special note of those categories, ranges or lines which produce a higher than average gross margin. To take sales figures alone as a check on performance can be misleading. Yet more sophistication can be built in by

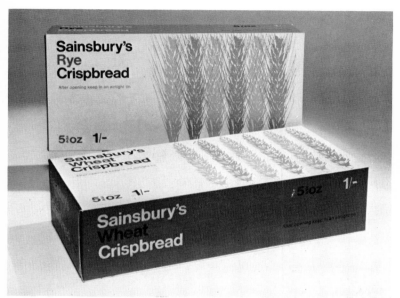

Plate 3   Sainsbury—Own Brand Pack.   *(Courtesy: Sainsbury)*

Plate 4   Sainsbury—Delivery Van.

discounting purchase tax which is, of course, non-profit making to the shop. These points are particularly important when dealing with lines such as greeting cards which may have a gross margin of over 40 per cent of retail selling price but which are taxed at 25 per cent.

Some research has been done in recent years, notably by Mead Carney, the management consultants, on the time factor in stock-holding. The mark-up or subsequent mark-down should, argue these consultants, be done in relation to the cost of keeping particular lines on the shelves. The problem of attributing overheads to each line is the most difficult aspect of this means of measuring profitability.

The locations of each department or category in a shop are also important for their bearing on sales and profit return. It is probable that impulse lines, e.g. tobacco, should be displayed at the front of the shop because if the product is not on sale in a part of the shop near the street, the shopper may go elsewhere. It also follows that non-impulse lines (i.e. those products which shoppers have to go to a particular shop for) can be handled towards the back of a shop. For instance, Boots Ltd, and other chemists very often locate the pharmacy section at the back of a shop with the result that shoppers are forced to go there for prescriptions, passing other displays on the way in and out. It is useful to experiment with department locations, particularly if there are local market peculiarities, monitoring the results of the change as compared with the previous layout. Ralph G. Towsey (in *Modern Merchandising*, see Bibliography) believes that there is still great scope for the 'trial and error' method of merchandising commodities in retail shops and, although this could be branded as being unscientific, there is much to be said for this approach so long as a set period is approved for trials so that after, say, 2 years all of a chain's branches are matched up to their market conditions.

Cash points must be planned at the layout stage; if registers are positioned on cash-and-wrap units this allows greater flexibility for future relays. Where there are a large number of exits, the cash-and-wrap system (which is allied to self-selection) is less secure than the checkout (self-service) system and also requires a higher labour content. All cash points should be clearly marked for customer convenience.

The type of shopfittings used must have some bearing on the problem of layout and display. The author would refer specifically to Mr Towsey's book (*idem*) for guidance on this particular aspect of display.

To summarise the last section, the branch layout which should be presented by the development manager for discussion with operating management should contain the following basics:

1 Linear wall and free standing footages to be allocated to each broad category of products.

H

2 Position of each category within the branch.
3 Position of cash points.
4 Layout of stockroom and ancillaries.
5 Type and number of fittings to be used with costs.

We now discuss various other aspects of branch planning which follow from the agreement of the layout plan.

COSTING

After the shop planner has produced a layout design for the new branch using the catalogue of standard fittings, a refined cost of fitting can then be calculated taking into account any building or other work which is necessary. (A quantity surveyor retained by the firm should have estimated those latter costs.) This final estimated cost can then be matched against tenders by shopfitting companies and builders which the estates department would now secure on the basis of the shop planner's layout. The tender finally accepted by the estates department on behalf of the company is then a budgeted cost and controls can be instituted. Some retail firms build in penalty clauses into contracts for tender stating that if completion is not achieved by an agreed date the contractor is liable to the retail company for any cash losses incurred. Time clauses and fixed price contracts tend to be loaded by the contractor for eventualities such as unforeseen delays due to shortage of skilled labour or materials.

STOCKING

We have already discussed some of the problems of allocating space to various commodities. This is partly allied to the stocking-out of a new branch and here we come across an inconsistency. In many trades, as has been explained, the ceiling turnover is not achievable for perhaps 2 or 3 years after opening. The problem here is to merchandise displays which will contain just sufficient stock for interim sales forecasts, but which will provide complete coverage in the shop to produce full and attractive displays. A measure of overstocking must occur, then, in some shops which have not yet reached their ultimate sales levels, but in this situation the stockroom should be relatively empty (except at peak trading times such as Christmas).

It is important when ordering merchandise for a new shop to base orders on viable stockturn information. This can initially be worked out by studying average stockturn for the chain as a whole. It is possible that particular market conditions may make for a deviation from the average in particular areas, but this can be picked up from EDP runs, model accounts or other performance monitors.

If shops are planned on a modular basis it is often possible to work out the cash value of stock per module or per foot run of display, as long as a large enough sample of shops is taken. For instance, 1 foot of display may contain £5·00 worth (at retail prices) of paperbacks or, conversely, £1·20 worth of canned soups. By grossing up the total display allocated to a particular category of goods a total stock figure can be deduced, and this figure will become more exact the larger the sample taken and the larger the individual display allocated to each category of commodity.

STAFFING

There are various methods of working out the staff establishment for a new branch.

1 *Sale per assistant* By dividing the total sales in chain branches by the total number of sales assistants employed (adding part timers together to make up full time assistants) an average sale per assistant can be gauged. This can range from £100 per week in efficient, small food shops (such as bakers) to over £200 per week in supermarkets.

2 *Wage percentage* If an average percentage of wages to total turn-over is taken, branches can be allowed up to a certain wage percentage, translated into cash terms, to employ a particular number of assistants. Wage percentages vary markedly from 4–5 per cent in the most efficient supermarkets to 15 per cent and more in small food and convenience food shops. For example in a shop taking £100,000 p.a. an 8 per cent wage percentage could be struck and if the average wage, including manager's salary, is £12 per week, the shop can afford to employ 12 or 13 full time staff.

This is to a certain degree an unsatisfactory method of apportioning staff to branches because the concept of a wage percentage can lead to inflexibility. By adhering strictly to a percentage there is a possibility of a reduction in service in certain branches. The sounder approach to staff establishments is to institute work studies of in-branch procedures. This is discussed in the following chapter.

Staffroom accommodation must, of course, be geared to the branch establishment, so that it conforms to the Offices, Shops and Railway Premises Act.

SERVICES AND STRUCTURE

Decisions must be made on the type of flooring, ceiling treatment, heating and ventilation equipment to be used and so on. These essential parts of the design of a branch may together constitute an overall image which the retailer is attempting to project.

COMMUNICATION

Certain persons and departments must be informed as to the progress of new branch planning. These are the:

1 Marketing director who should receive a monthly progress report from the development manager.

2 Operating management including the general manager, the area manager and the branch manager designate who should be involved at the shop planning and layout stage and who would make suggestions and amendments under most of the headings listed in this section.

3 Merchandising manager who might be involved in some stock ordering and in the advertising of the new branch in the Press. The merchandising manager would also be involved in the planning of any opening or special promotions in the new branch.

4 Retail accountant who would be involved in arranging initial floats, opening a local bank account, allocating a computer code to the branch, liaising with the computer section on staff wages and so on.

See Appendix II for a checklist for pre-planning a new shop project.

PHASING

The shop opening schedule is the plan by which the development department programmes the shop opening. The estates department would also phase their operations in line with this schedule. The branch opening manager should produce a phasing programme with dates for each individual project and this can be usefully backed up by charting progress on a 'Sasco' or similar planner.

THE SHOP OPENING SCHEDULE

In most retail trades a 10–12 week opening programme is quite acceptable provided that the pre-planning outlined in the preceding pages has been followed. A full opening schedule is given in Appendix III.

IMPLEMENTATION

The previous sections have described the pre-planning which must occur before the branch enters the last stage of its progress towards opening. After the branch has been handed over in an acceptable state by the estates department to the operators, the branch opening manager begins his main work which is set out in the shop opening schedule referred to. On opening day the branch is then the total responsibility of the operating management.

CHECKS

Apart from monitoring the new branch's performance (development department) the estates department should organise an on-site meeting say 3 months after opening with representatives from the shopfitters and operating management present so that any minor problems which have arisen since the branch began trading can be discussed and solved. Any serious problems such as leaking roofs or dangerous fittings must, of course, be dealt with as soon as they arise.

SOURCES AND REFERENCES

1 *Productivity and Capital Expenditure in Retailing.* K. D. George and P. V. Hills. C.U.P., 1968.

7
IMPROVING BRANCH RESULTS

The basic intention of this book is to illustrate the possibilities open to retail management for improving the profitability of their companies. The book deals with overall plans for creating better organisation, more viable markets, more attractive and meaningful corporate identities and so on. At the core of all retailing effort, however, is the branch and in this unit lie the real possibilities for the ultimate success or failure of the company. This chapter can therefore be regarded as a key one which deals with the main factors influencing individual branch performance, and attempts to indicate some guidelines for action to improve profitability.

OPPORTUNITIES AND PROBLEMS

Too often one hears retailers discussing the 'problems' of particular branches: consistent net losses, lack of suitable staff, growing competition, inadequate maintenance and so forth. The more positive term 'opportunities' is less often heard: the *planned* extension of a branch to meet consistently increasing sales; the successful creation of a local demand, the forced closure of inefficient competition and so on. As Peter Drucker has emphasised it is more profitable in the longer term to concentrate on the opportunity areas, rather than to invest time and money in the weak areas of performance. Nothing could be more true of retailing. The first step is to try to isolate the problem and the opportunity areas in individual branch operation. Informed decisions can then be made to increase profitability by taking advantage of changing external conditions and by more effective mobilisation of resources. It is obvious that management cannot take meaningful action without accurate information. The next section of this chapter therefore deals with the factual and statistical requirements for decision taking at branch level.

INFORMATION SOURCES

It is not the author's intention to discuss in any great detail the conventional sources of information available to the retailer from his accounting systems, as these are exhaustively discussed in many excellent books, some of which are listed in the Bibliography at the end of this book. A brief summary of sources, however, is as follows:

I TRADING/PROFIT AND LOSS ACCOUNT

This account, which may be published for units as regularly as each week or as irregularly as once a year contains information on sales and on the costs of making these sales. Apart from the sales total, the gross and net profits produced in the account are the two important control figures, the former because a change in the mix of goods sold may change the average gross margin and the latter because certain costs may have altered to produce a different net profit. Ideally, the trading account should contain columns which detail either the comparative figures for the period previous or better still, budget/model figures which act as targets or forecasts to compare with actual performance. With comparative information readily available, any changes in performance can be isolated and interpreted. Some form of monitoring system is desirable when a large number of accounts are produced at any one time, perhaps by computer printouts programmed on an exception basis. (Such information should include number of customers, sales per assistant, weekly cash statement, etc.)

2 UNIT BALANCE SHEET

A total of net assets employed in each branch should be produced annually and kept up to date. When this capital figure is matched with the net profit figure for the period, a return on capital employed percentage is available. This capital figure is extremely useful as the basis for project appraisal, any further investments of capital to be invested in the branch (such as new fittings) being added to the estimated figure and the projected increase in net profit flowing from the new investment being now measureable in ROCE terms. In other words, the contribution that fixed assets make to units and company performance is now open to investigation.

3 SALES MIX

There are various methods of producing a breakdown of sales by department, range or line. This can be done through periodic stock-takes, by recording cash register totals (where appropriate), by 'tagging' merchandise or by physical recording of items at the cash point. Whatever form this monitoring takes and to what depth the information is recorded, every retailer should have sales mix information for specific and comparable periods to hand.

4 STOCKHOLDING

Periodic stocktakes are the best monitor of stock levels per department, range or line as this will determine shrinkage figures, although some retail firms like Mothercare with fully computerised stock ordering systems do not take physical stocks but prefer to rely on Kimball tags. By matching sales per commodity (sales mix) with stock levels a stock-turn can be calculated; this may not be identical for each commodity in each branch, but should be a viable basis for formulating standard or budgeted stockholding.

5 DISPLAY ALLOCATION

The organisation of each branch in terms of the space allocated to open displays of various departments or sub-categories should be known. Because the sales mix and the gross margins available from each commodity are calculated the matching of the total gross profit flowing from a commodity with the space allocated to its display will then show how usefully, in gross profit terms, the available space in each branch is being organised.

6 MARKET INFORMATION

Briefly, the type of data required falls under three main heads:

1 COMPETITION Any changes in local competition can have an effect on the sales level of a branch.

2 GENERAL SHOPPING Changes in the shopping environment, e.g. the resiting of a major multiple can also affect branch fortunes.

3 LOCAL PLANNING This covers traffic management schemes, re-development of shopping and so on, again carrying the potential for changes in branch performance.

These latter aspects are discussed more fully elsewhere but the ideal channel of information is through the branch manager to head office, usually by means of a weekly report.

The sort of information described above which should be available on branch performance will enable management to isolate the opportunity and/or problem areas, preferably on an exception basis. The problems are likely to flow from one or both of two sources, namely management (at any level, but mostly at branch level) and the market. It can be argued that even problems caused by changes in the external environment are really the result of poor management planning and forecasting, but this is not in any large respect true. The opportunities are likely to flow from changing market situations only and (by the same token as above) not from management activity. In order to delineate the management aspect of problem solving more fully the next section deals with the functions of management at branch level.

BRANCH MANAGEMENT FUNCTIONS

In a retail business the branch manager is the keystone around which profitability is built. Planning done at head office level with direct relevance to shop operation cannot be fully implemented without both the competence and agreement of the branch management force.

One of the problems in any discussion of the function of a branch manager is that of the varying degrees of autonomy which retail firms allow at this level of management. Some firms have tended in the past to attract poor quality branch management, basically because of low salary scales, a situation still endemic in many parts of the industry. Such firms are often insufficiently organised centrally to offer the strong guidance and control which low competence levels require. In the author's view, because of the relative geographical isolation of retail branch management, compared with other industries, a large measure of direct control from a central office is desirable although this might conflict with different market requirements in various parts of the country. If these differing market conditions are strong enough to affect overall profitability, as they might in certain aspects of the retail food and garment trades, then cognizance must be taken of them. In a properly controlled retail organisation these particularities are, of course, monitored and the branches stocked with appropriate goods. The effects on profitability of reaction or otherwise to known market differences are also measurable.

To return to the branch manager's functions, the broad purpose of his job is to ensure the efficient and profitable operation of his branch. To carry out this task successfully he must be aware of the detailed factors which can improve or weaken the performance of his branch. By this it is not meant that he should be totally responsible for correcting in-store weaknesses and improving his overall branch performance, but he should be competent enough to isolate the strengths and weaknesses of his situation and bring them, where appropriate, to the attention of his area manager or supervisor. Each branch manager should, in the author's view, know what is expected of him in the performance of the branch under his control and should be conversant with the relationship between sales, gross surplus earned and the expenses incurred in achieving these sales. He should therefore be aware of the potential of the branch for sales development, the comparative gross profitabilities of the products he is selling, the expenses which must be charged against his gross profit and be alive to the importance of his net profit return.

The most important parts of a branch manager's job are set out below.

1 PROFITABILITY

To achieve planned levels of profit both gross and net, for the period. The plan is founded on a model or, more strictly, a budget profit and loss account which is likely to be based on the previous period's accounts, but allowing for any changes in margins and operating costs (it is difficult to forecast any future changes in sales mix which might affect overall gross in a particular branch).

2 SALES

To achieve budgeted sales for the period. This can be measured on a rolling basis using a moving annual total of sales or by comparing one 52 week financial year with another. Some firms budget for a particular percentage increase in sales which will take in price rises and also show a 'real' increase in sales (say 5 per cent). If sales in a branch have shown a decrease over a long period it is realistic to budget for a further decrease if investigations show that the downturn is due to market conditions outside the retailer's control, rather than to in-store weaknesses that are correctable.

3 COSTS

To maintain costs within budget. This really means that the branch manager must keep all controllable expenses within his budget. If a wage increase is suddenly granted after budgets have been prepared this is not strictly a controllable expense. There is, however, no excuse for property rent reviews not being incorporated in budgets, and in this particular case a liaison between the budget framers and the estates department is necessary.

4 STOCK

To control stocks at a budgeted cash figure sufficient to support the planned sales of the branch. The stock figure is likely to vary according to the seasonal sales trends and a more sophisticated approach to stock budgeting is to incorporate seasonal stock levels within the budget rather than to control by accepting a maximum variance of actual stock to standard stock throughout the year.

5 LOSSES

To keep trading losses to a minimum. This aspect of a manager's control function covers shrinkage and stock depreciation.

The above five aspects of a branch manager's function can be quantified in budget form, as has been shown, but they should also be agreed by the manager with his senior to ensure full and enthusiastic participation. It follows then, as previously discussed, that the branch manager must be fully conversant not only with the budget documents but with the reasoning behind the figures. This requires a certain amount of formal training which should not be handed out on the shopfloor by the manager's senior, but should be incorporated in head office or regional training schemes. To continue with other aspects of the branch manager's task.

6 BUYING

To ensure that all orders (or purchases) are made in line with company policy for that grade of branch. If issues to branches are not controlled centrally, some control must be put on the branch manager as to the type of lines he is allowed to order and from which suppliers. He should also be issued with open-to-buy instructions. This situation can be controlled by issuing a catalogue of suppliers and lines to each branch and notifying the appropriate suppliers of each branch's approved range. This method of buying control, however, not only places a considerable amount of work on the suppliers' shoulders but orders have additionally to be checked by the branch manager's seniors. For certain food, tobacco and confectionery lines, direct supplies from the manufacturer are acceptable because of the relative efficiency of the distributive system, but for many other commodities a central warehouse is probably the best solution in that, properly controlled, it can guarantee speed of supply and firm grip on branch ordering. Such an operation should, ideally, be directly controlled by the marketing department of the retail firm in liaison with the trading department.

7 STAFF

To ensure that the branch is properly staffed to meet trading requirements. As long as a branch is up to its agreed establishment, this falls primarily into the budget category when the wage complement in operating costs is kept to an agreed percentage. Secondary but perhaps more pressing problems for the branch manager are to see that:

1 All staff employed are of the highest standard available having regard to the wage scale offered and market conditions.

2 Staff turnover does not exceed a maximum; the author knows of one supermarket company that consistently turned over its entire sales staff once a year and higher levels are not unknown in retailing. This problem is, of course, associated with wage scales, conditions of service, company morale and other factors, apart from the general conditions in the labour market for all grades and industries.

3 All new staff receive instruction and training. Experienced staff should also undergo periodic refresher courses, or entirely new courses when special ranges or modified in-store fitting have been introduced. Some of this training can be done by the branch manager at regular intervals, but specialist training, for example of the Training Within Industry type, must be carried out at regional or head office level.

8 ADMINISTRATION

To carry out all clerical and security operations in line and company policy in that:

1 All required records are kept up to date.
2 All periodic and 'one-off' returns are received by head office when required.
3 Company instructions regarding the security of cash, stock and premises are observed.

9 DISPLAY

To maintain standards of display which encourage and retain trade and contribute to the identity which the company wishes to project in that:

1 Sales area windows and shopfront are maintained in a clean and tidy condition (this would also apply to stock area, restrooms, toilets, etc.).
2 All stock is displayed in line with the company standards: this would include the open display of all lines appropriate to the grade of branch, the correct price marking and ticketing of products, the retention of agreed displays, merchandised appropriately and so on.
3 Displays are prepared to take advantage of head office promotions and special events.

The foregoing nine basic functions of a branch manager are controllable either through a budget or through a branch operating manual which should lay down the standards of performance acceptable to the company particularly in the areas of staff, administration and display. Once standards of performance and competence have been published, monitoring can be carried out through exception reports on sales and profit performance and by physical inspections; a checklist of items is useful and when filled in by the supervisor or area manager can be discussed with the branch manager. Consistent breach of the standards laid down by the company would, of course, represent a problem which may or may not be the responsibility of the branch manager. Dirty fittings are not usually excusable, but dirt filtering into a shop due to the need for maintenance, for instance, would be the responsibility of more senior management (assuming that the branch manager has reported it).

Having seen what a branch manager is responsible for, we can now go on to attempt an examination of those areas of shop performance by the manager and those areas which are strictly outside his control. It will be seen that, in practice, there are few clearcut distinctions between the controllable and the uncontrollable as far as the branch manager is concerned and that much of a branch's strengths and weaknesses flow directly from the policy and planning functions of head office. A few factors are not even open to influence from the centre but, by and large, the success or failure of a retail chain is in the hands of its board of management. This is not to say that a manager himself cannot make a tangible contribution to branch performance by good shopkeeping, but his efforts are, as explained, limited by external circumstances.

We now detail several broad factors, discussed at length, which may affect the performance of the individual branch.

LOCATION MONITORS

In a review of the author's previous book, David Jones of *The Times* Business News suggested that: 'A detailed study of just what has made one site profitable and another a white elephant is long overdue, and there is a book to be written analysing the choice of sites as a factor in the comparative success or failure of some of our major multiple groups.' Such a book would undoubtedly be of great interest to retailers and other businessmen but this particular aspect of retailing is so poorly documented on an inter-firm basis that a book on it is unlikely ever—unfortunately—to be written. A further difficulty is the isolating of the siting factor from other factors which influence branch performance. Bearing in mind Mr Jones's suggestion, however, the author presents later in this chapter a number of case studies which attempt to illustrate particular aspects of success and failure at branch level.

There are many reasons for inadequate unit performances. The most important of these, in the author's view, is the skimping of market appreciation and a resulting poor project appraisal. If this is accepted, it follows that the problems facing both new and established shops revolve basically around their markets. It is perhaps useful to discuss new and established outlets separately because the acquisition of a new branch is normally a quite deliberate act of policy which can either be changed or forestalled in its execution. The problems of the inadequate established branch are, as it were, with the retailer from the start, the only solution in many cases being disposal. No retailer, of course, wishes to dispose of a brand new outlet a few years or months after acquisition. These things, however, happen.

NEW BRANCHES

Location   A shop badly related to its market and to other traders cannot draw on the potential of a well sited branch. Occasionally, shops are opened in areas where there is no present or future market potential. A proper market appraisal of pedestrian flows and catchment area must be carried out so that either the correct site is bought or the location is rejected. Although the author has in the past come down strongly against the 'intuitive' approach to site selection, there is still much to be said for sensing the rightness of a location for particular trades. The market research analysis which is now to a far greater extent done during retail site investigations is, in many cases, carried out purely to back up someone's instinct for or against a project. This is self-evident in many other industries where capital commitments have to be made.

Competition   Severe competition from retail traders in the same line of business can, again, ruin a site's potential. This aspect of site selection would, of course, be dealt with in the general market survey. The likelihood of further competitive shops opening within the catchment area should also be studied, but if an optimum level of competition is apparent other competing firms keep out. What an 'optimum' level is depends on the particular trade and on the experience of the site assessor, carefully comparing the location under study with similar situations elsewhere. Quantification is almost impossible. The presence of competing shops in certain trades, however (e.g. shoe and electrical shops, variety chains and supermarkets), can attract more outlets in the same trade, particularly in town centres where, sometimes, whole sections of streets are devoted to one retail trade.

Size of unit   A shop which is physically too large for its market may fail because the gross profit flowing from a relatively low sales level may not be sufficient to pay operating costs such as rent and rates. A shop too small for its market may lose sales because of overcrowding.

Budgeting   Faulty estimates stem from an incorrect sales forecast, either in total or in mix. One of the most common errors retailers fall into is to over-estimate potential sales. This, in many cases, is the result of under-estimating the strength of competition but, as suggested above, this is not a mistake which is easily avoided. The accurate estimation of competitive potential can be much more difficult than calculating the total catchment area expenditure. Some retailers still estimate a new shop's potential by a straight comparison between existing branch sales in one shopping centre and the possibilities in what they believe to be a similar situation. Unfortunately, no two retail situations are alike, and the development department can only go some way towards solving the comparison problem by grading outlets by sales and product mix and relating this to shopping centre type.

EXISTING BRANCHES

Location As previously stated, the relationship of a branch to its market is crucial. If there occurs a change in the environment, this may have an effect on the performance of the branch. Market changes may occur through many factors, including the following:

1 POPULATION Increases or decreases in catchment area population and changes in population mix (i.e. social classes and their potential expenditure).

2 COMMUNICATION Changes in car parking accommodation, traffic management schemes, rerouting of bus services, changes in bus stop locations, pedestrian crossings, crash barriers and so on can markedly alter the number of pedestrians (potential shoppers) passing particular points in and around shopping centres.

3 REDEVELOPMENT Changes brought about by renewal, extension or resiting schemes for shopping centres.

4 AMENITY Urban renewal can also produce better environmental conditions for shopping, by providing better services or just by planting trees and providing open spaces.

5 MULTIPLE RETAILERS Changes in location by important (magnet) retailers can affect for good or ill the performances of other traders in the vicinity.

Competition An increase (or decrease) in the level of competition can also affect branch results. One well known supermarket chain's branches were regularly affected in initial stages by the opening of branches in the same vicinity of an equally well known chain basically because double or treble trading stamps were offered by the latter for a 2–3 week period after opening; this could bring about a fall of as much as 15–20 per cent in sales in the former chain's branches, for this initial period. Other types of competition are often far less ostensible, but much more difficult to isolate and quantify in terms of branch performance. There are a number of methods by which competition can be fought by a retailer faced with it and the methods are discussed more fully later in this chapter.

Size of unit Branches which have too much or too little sales area for their market invariably have to be closed eventually because of the pressure on costs in the former case or the pressure on space in the latter. The case studies described later in this chapter help to illustrate this particular problem.

Budgeting Normally a standard increase in sales would be budgeted for each year (say 6–10 per cent) in each branch and, naturally, increases in costs should also be budgeted, e.g. at rent reviews. Occasionally, due to an increase in certain costs a branch becomes uneconomic and this is particularly so when the cost increases are not matched by a comparative increase in sales and gross profit. Cost increases in branches are also dealt with later in this chapter.

The foregoing problems with regard to location and project appraisal are now discussed in six case studies which, because they are largely textual, are treated as an integral part of the book and not as an appendix.

SIX LOCATION CASE STUDIES

Most books and articles written on retail subjects in this country appear to rely heavily on general statements of practice or on theoretical assumptions which are strictly unproved in their texts, particularly with regard to the problem of retail siting. In the next section, the author attempts to illustrate through six case studies the type of problems which retailers have actually faced after selecting particular sites.

CASE STUDY I

A retail bakery multiple took a standard unit in the main street of a medium sized Midlands town. The street contained old properties but was well filled with the normal complement of national multiples. The new shop was fitted out in the current style of the bakery multiple and, along with a small catering section, was expected to turn over £450 per week.

On the basis of this sales estimate, the following costings were done:

Sales

	Shop	Coffee bar	Total
Estimated weekly sales	£350	100	450
Cost of supplies	£220	40	260
Gross profit	£130	60	190

Weekly operating costs

Rent and rates	£50		
Wages	£45		
General expenses (including delivery, waste, depreciation on fittings, heat and light, etc.)	£35	(total)	130

Estimated weekly net profit £60

Break-even point was calculated at total weekly sales of £320, split £260 to shop and £60 to coffee bar and by apportioning appropriate operating costs to each of the two sections of the shop.

It had been estimated that the shop would open at a total sales level of £250 per week and rise after 6 months to £300 and would be breaking even within 1 year, reaching its optimum sales level after 2 years.

The shop/coffee bar actually opened for trading at an average level of £200 and rose slowly to £250 per week after 9 months and then stayed at this level for some considerable time afterwards.

All types of sales boosting methods were tried to increase sales but the main problem was insoluble. The shop was sited within a street without any other retail food support except a small multiple grocer 100 yards away (the food sections in the nearby variety chains could not, in this particular instance, be regarded as support). Although pedestrian flows at the site had been checked by area management before the unit was taken, and apparently found satisfactory, the shoppers using the street were not primarily engaged in food shopping during this particular part of their round. Some simple market research could possibly have established this, but the mistake was one which could have been avoided by following the well known dictum that food shops should locate together to gain the associated sales which flow from such complementary locations.

CASE STUDY 2

A well known and very successful supermarket chain located in a south London suburb which contained a medium sized shopping centre with two much larger regional centres within 5 miles radius.

The unit had to be extended within a quite short time of opening because the market study upon which the branch size was calculated was found to be faulty in that the catchment area, which had been drawn in a constricted fashion to take account of the two neighbouring major shopping centres (only one of which, incidentally, contained a branch of the company), did not take into account in certain sections of its periphery the customer loyalty to this particular supermarket chain. A subsequent more comprehensive market survey which pinpointed those areas from which customers were travelling to shop at the branch

117

I

made this abundantly clear. The convention that support for a super-market diminishes quite radically at each successive mile radius from the site was found not to be generally applicable to this particular supermarket company and since then, in common with the large super-market companies, the average size of this company's retail branches has increased by over 50 per cent in sales areas.)

CASE STUDY 3

A newsagent, bookseller and stationer opened a branch in a northern town of 70,000 local authority population.

The sales area of the branch was rather less than 1000 ft² and esti-mated sales were £72,000 per annum. Although tobacco, confectionery and newspapers (no deliveries) were expected to make up to 50 per cent of this, the shop was incapable of physically containing this sales level, particularly at seasonal peaks. This was established after examining accounts in comparable branches in the chain where the average annual sales per (net) square foot was £40.

	£	£
Annual sales		72,000
Notional gross profit (24 per cent)		17,280
Less Rent and rates	3,750	
Wages	7,200	
General expenses	2,500	(total) 13,450
Annual net profit		3,830
Capital costs were computed as follows:		
Building and shopfitting	9,000	
Stock (at cost)	10,000	
	19,000	

Some time after opening, with sales at £600–700 per week, i.e. some-what less than half the estimate, building and fitting costs rose by a further £2000 making a further charge to capital depreciation and increasing the rent cost (the extra building costs were, of course, rentalised).

After less than 18 months trading it was recognised that the branch would never become profitable because:

1 The budgeted sales figure was unattainable in this size of shop.
2 The pitch was declining.
3 The high cost of making the shop suitable for the trade in re-building and fitting out was punishing.

It was therefore decided to resite the branch in a new precinct which had attracted several well known multiples, many of them in large units. The new unit size was 2000 ft² trading on one floor and the budgeted sales figure was £100,000. (It is interesting to note here that the original sales forecast was an under-estimate for the town, but the site selected for carrying out the trade was, as explained, unsuitable.) The resited branch moved quickly past its break-even point and reached its sales target within 2 years of opening.

CASE STUDY 4

A multiple ladies' clothing shop opened in a northern town of 100,000 population with a ground-floor sales area of 1000 ft² and a first floor sales area of 3000 ft². Although the original sales estimate is unknown to the author he estimates it in excess of £100,000 p.a. After some years of trading sales were still only £50,000 p.a. and the decision was taken to close the branch. What had not been fully recognised at the siting stage was that, as the company operated two very large shops in a big regional centre 10 miles away and local women were more inclined to travel to this large centre which also offered a comprehensive range of competitive ladies wear shops, this particular branch suffered as a result. The location was run down and offered very few clothing shops catering for this particular segment of the female market. The branch was too large to carry out this particular trade, was not achieving its budgeted turnover and, as a result, was loss making having regard to the rental (£6500 p.a.) and the lack of gross profit flowing from the low sales figure.

CASE STUDY 5

A South Coast chemist decided to open a second branch in a busy district centre in a large town in order to attempt to trap custom which was not using his central shop. The new shop was excellently sited between a well known supermarket company's branch and a prosperous independent baker (with bakehouse to rear). It was fitted out for self-selection in 1000 ft² of sales area and the chemist forecast with the help of a marketing consultant friend a sales level after 3 years of £1000 per week. This target was achieved just over 2 years after opening producing budgeted gross profit of £14,000. He employed a qualified pharmacist and six assistants, including two part timers and budgeted his wage percentage at 7 per cent. He found, however, that he had to pay over scale to retain assistants in this particular area and had not foreseen that his off-licence section, which became very popular due to lack of competition, required one full timer and one part timer almost continuously to run it. He also experienced a shrinkage rate, mostly attributable to theft by staff and customers of 3 per cent. The forecast and actual operating costs compared as follows:

	Forecast £		Actual £	
Annual gross profit		14,000		14,000
Less Rent and rates	3,000		3,000	
Wages	3,500		4,500	
General expenses	2,000	8,500	3,000	10,500
Annual net profit		5,500		3,500

His return on capital of £14,000 therefore shrank from an estimated 39 per cent to an actual of 25 per cent where he had opened the shop to achieve at least 30 per cent ROCE.

He was fortunately able to acquire the independent baker's business next door and created a fully self-service operation (except, of course, for the dispensary) which tapped further demand in the area and created a situation where his wage costs and losses rose less than proportionately to sales and were catered for more adequately by a higher (cash) gross profit.

CASE STUDY 6

A small grocery cash-and-carry operator in the West Country was offered as repayment of a debt a run down grocer's shop in a secondary position in a prosperous West Country town. The gentleman concerned accepted the business and decided to run it as a delicatessen shop. He was able without much structural alteration to open the shop to trade on 900 ft², as a basically counter service operation selling delicatessen products and allied lines. He purchased three gondolas and stocked them with high class canned goods for which cash was taken at an auxiliary checkout at the front of the shop.

Sales were not particularly buoyant, at £25,000 during the first full year's trading against a budget of £35,000. This was mainly due to competition from existing counter service grocers. A slow uplift in sales continued, but the operation was loss making (no factual details available). The delicatessen owner then contacted a small multiple baker who agreed to take a concession in one half of the shop, on a counter service basis. The baker was able to merchandise an excellent range of fresh cream fancies along with meat pastry products and, happily, due to the discernment of local shoppers the dual operation, which was skillfully advertised, increased total sales within 2 full years to £45,000 (split £33,000 to the delicatessen lines and the balance on bakery and confectionery lines). The delicatessen owner was particularly fortunate to have secured a sympathetic retail trade with which to share his operation.

Table 7.1 illustrates the six studies. The main points to be picked out of them are discussed below.

TABLE 7.1 Six siting case studies

Case study	Prime error in assessment	Sequential error(s)	Result	Actual/possible action
1 Baker	Wrong site	(a) Sales forecast too high for location (b) Costings wrong	Loss maker	Closure and resite
2 Supermarket	Sales forecast too low	Unit too small	Crowded branch and possible loss of sales to competition	Branch extension
3 Newsagent	Unit too small	(a) Sales forecast too high for unit (b) Costings wrong	Loss maker	Closure and resite
4 Ladieswear	Sales forecast too high	Unit too large	Loss-maker	Closure
5 Chemist	Wrong costings	Unacceptable ROCE	Realised profit lower than budgeted net	Branch extension
6 Delicatessen	Unit too large	Sales forecast too high: competition not properly assessed	Loss maker	Concession to complementary trader

A thread of logic runs through all these case studies except number 3 which is in many ways a most interesting inconsistency. But first let us discuss the common mistakes which were perpetrated in the other five.

COMMON ASSESSMENT ERRORS

Wrong siting There are certain rules (which are often broken by the more successful retailers) as to the location of new shops. These are dealt with elsewhere in this book and very fully in the author's previous work *Retail Site Assessment*.

Over-optimistic sales forecasts This is the most common error in siting. Many retailers tend to be over-optimistic and discount competition. The straight comparison of another branch in a similar location is not necessarily the basis for a sound budget forecast. Some further research into the catchment or market area must be undertaken.

Pessimistic sales forecasts This is the least common error and one which many retailers would perhaps wish to make, if not continually. This type of mistake can be costly (but not as costly as closing a branch) in the extension or renting which must eventually come.

Incorrect cost budgets Mistakes in estimating operating costs can occur in several ways. Some of the information upon which the budget is based may be nebulous, e.g. wage cost estimates or budgeted sales mix (which if wrong can produce a different gross profit margin). Mistakes of this kind have even been tracked down to mathematical error.

To return to case study 3, the inconsistency here is obvious. The estimate of sales took no apparent account of the average sales per square foot likely to be achieved in a successful small newsagents shop (about £40 per square foot per annum excluding news deliveries). On the basis of the £72,000 p.a. estimate the shop should have been twice the size it was (1800 ft²). The branch in fact took £40 per square foot but traded at half the budgeted sales figure. The error here was to ignore the internal data readily available in the company before the site was contracted for. In the other cases, the retail companies had to rely on external data referring to the site *qua* site which is obviously far more difficult to collect and quantify.

MERCHANDISING

We have dealt in the previous section with some of the problems associated with the locational aspects of marketing in new and existing branches. Now we must consider the marketing opportunities and problems presented by the in-store environment. This discussion centres around the products and means of presenting them.

Let us first discuss the basic goals towards which the merchandising effort of retailers should be directed. For convenience, the following headings are used:

1 Increasing profitable sales.
2 Increasing stockturn.
3 Presentation.

1 INCREASING PROFITABLE SALES

Local market opportunities The most obvious method of monitoring the branch's ability to take advantage of local market opportunities is by examining the sales pattern. If sales are increasing this is undoubtedly due to one or other of the factors described elsewhere (increasing population, closure of competition, increased popularity of the shopping centre, etc.). Such increases are passive but, more constructively, increased sales can be produced by taking from competition. This can be done quite expensively by increasing the range of goods carried, by price cutting, by advertising and sales promotional devices and so on. It is never cheap to 'poach' sales off a competitor, and the retailer must look at the costs of securing the extra sales against the extra gross margin he produces. Local market opportunities may provide short term gains but are unlikely to provide long term benefits unless there has occurred an environmental change as has been described previously. It has often been suggested that a decrease in an individual branch sales has been due to the refit of a competitor and it has been further suggested that competition can only be combated by a branch refit (costing, say, £5000). This would mean an extra £10 per week required on gross profit to pay for the refit alone. In order to give a minimum (20 per cent) return on capital this could involve retailers in an extra £30–60 per week on their sales which with the smaller butchery or bakery outlets is a considerable (up to 20 per cent) increase. Mere pressure from competition does not merit large-scale investment, which should only be made if there is likely to be an increase in the total market. Local competition should be viewed on its merits. If it is strong enough to take away 50 per cent and more of a department or range, then it is probably not worth fighting on its own terms, assuming that the retail branch suffering is average or better in its operation. This is not to say that competition should be ignored. The very fact that competition is effective should be a spur to the retailer to conquer it as soon as its influence is felt, by carrying out competition checks on merchandise, shopfitting, staffing, etc. and making such changes in one's own branch as is thought fit. The real answer is to spot gaps in competitors' ranges and fill them, but this is difficult for a multiple on a central buying system. Any fighting of competition must, of course, be done broadly within the firm's ability and inclination to fight.

Range appraisal The end product of correct merchandising is to stock a mix of goods which will create a gross profit flow large enough to pay operating costs and leave a residue substantial enough either to return the target reward on capital invested or otherwise to satisfy the owner of the business for his risk. The implication here is that the merchandise stocked and its control will also satisfy the customer and create customer loyalty. In order to progress, these ranges must be appraised in general line within the sales they exhibit in the branches. In addition it is possible that under the general trading up which has occurred in retailing during the past 10 years that the firm may wish to buy stock which offers the best gross profit return, having regard to the need to carry ranges of a certain comprehensiveness in line with the agreed image of the company. Appraisal of stock should also be in line with the sales mix of the firm as computed through the normal channels, and the lower end of the scale tackled for 'passenger' lines. One bakery group recently made an appraisal of cake sales per company and found that several dozen lines were selling at a rate of less than £5 per outlet per week. This would mean a gross contribution of less than £2 from this line per week towards individual branch overheads. It is occasionally agreed that loss of variety can lose custom, but the argument as Professor McClelland has said: 'Cutting them out may lose some customers who bought other things as well, but some . . . will be made up by sales of other products in their place.'[1] As some lines are cut out, more space is allowable for extending better selling lines, and this is true of stock space, stockturn, the whole reducing general cost.

Stock assortment should reflect market demands if they can be assessed. Local markets are difficult to investigate and many multiples may not wish to alter their central buying procedures to take account of local demands. In the food trades it is sometimes imperative. For instance, pickled onions in malt vinegar are acceptable in London while white vinegar is not, this being more popular in the Midlands. Apart from local tastes in food there are subtle physical differences, for instance, between the average woman in Scotland and that in the South of England: a slightly larger cup size is demanded in brassieres in Scotland than in London. Some arbitrary percentage, say 2–3, should be taken as the minimum of total gross profit that any line should contribute to a range, or any range to a category of products or a department. New products should also be screened for acceptability and total gross profit contribution in local markets. A classic case occurred some years ago when an issue of women's paper pants was made to the branch of a national multiple in a small town in the North of Scotland. They were not acceptable, though whether because of the climate or the local *mores* was not researched.

Voluntary customer panels and 'want slips' are other methods of identifying local market needs while market research, although expensive, has produced some interesting reports on food and clothing purchases.

If a trading-up operation is considered necessary the lines selected should offer the best gross profit return, having regard to the need to carry ranges of certain comprehensiveness in line with the agreed image of the company. Certain towns allow this and in Norwich a national multiple managed a (notional) extra 2–3 per cent on its gross margin through careful stock selection when the branch was opened.

In addition the marketing department of the retail firm should be investigating the potential of current growth markets with particular emphasis, where appropriate, on local market conditions. If it is decided to merchandise a range of, say, motor accessories the branches issued with them should have their trading areas canvassed beforehand by area managers to sound out the local competition, in this case garage fore-court kiosks, motor enthusiasts' shops and other multiples and department stores carrying such a range. Any new ranges should also be sympathetic with other products being sold in the branches.

British Home Stores, a case in point, have during the last few years deliberately aimed at a particular sector of the retail market, somewhere between Marks and Spencer and Woolworth. This has been engineered by a tough range appraisal in which 9000 lines have been pruned by more than half. This has naturally meant the weeding out of some fast moving lines and the concentration on textiles which account for about 60 per cent of sales. The philosophy behind this is to extend displays of picked lines until they reach a point where marginal returns disappear. If some parity can be achieved in the sales per counter foot between lines—and this is fairly easy to achieve in a product group such as gloves—then an automatic check on overdisplay can be produced.[2]

Merchandising a carefully picked range of goods can be advantageous; buying problems are immediately reduced as is stockholding, display, pricing and accounting. On the other hand, a poor appraisal of the market initially can have disastrous results.

There is no doubt that the carrying of a large number of lines can reduce a chain's total profitability and old lines should be dropped when new come in. Poor screening of sales can hide large areas in the range where stock is not moving at all.

Sales promotion and advertising The adequate promotion by in-store showcards and manufacturers selling aids, window posters and press advertising is, of course, useful for increasing sales levels, as are trading stamps, free gifts, 'specials', loss leaders and the many other methods of promotion used in retail shops today. Under this heading we may mention bonus schemes for branch managers and staff and inter-branch competitions based on shop leagues.

There are certain fundamentals which must be borne in mind when selecting goods for sales promotion:

1 Promotion must benefit the shop's complete turnover and not merely increase sales of one commodity at the expense of another.
2 The item to be promoted must be of a nature to respond.
3 The retailer must be fully aware of the increase in sales required to maintain the same gross profit on an item which has been marked down.
4 When assessing the benefit from a promotion the extra costs of it must be offset against the extra gross profit derived.
5 Too many promotions at one time defeat their object.

2 INCREASING STOCKTURN

Stocks can be reduced and average stockturn increased by weeding out slow moving and/or unprofitable lines. Stock is the most profit creative of all capital investment in retail shops, if properly controlled. By optimising this resource a stock level can be reached, taking into account seasonal changes in sales pattern, which will support the expected sales levels and no more, i.e. stockturn will be optimum. There are, of course, a large number of different stockturns in a branch—as many as there are lines—and by reducing the number of slow sellers the average can be hoisted, but this must be done with some eye to the margins which each line produces. As part of the marketing strategy of the firm, planned buying should take place in line with company objectives so that the planned (or notional) gross margin is achieved as far as possible by securing a stock assortment whereby high and low margin lines together produce the overall desired margin and the corporate identity of the firm is enhanced.

Gordon Selfridge's dictum that the good shopkeeper (or merchandiser) provides the right goods in the right place at the right time in the right manner in the right quantities and at the right price is still as valid today as when it was first formulated. It is also as meaningless as the famous definition of democracy attributed to Lincoln until it is translated into a tangible situation containing the problems of stock lead times, efficiency of supplies, deliveries, etc.

Good stock presentation can also aid the speeding up of stockturn.

3 PRESENTATION

The basic rules which should govern this aspect of branch merchandising are now discussed.

Display allocation This has been discussed elsewhere in this book and assumes that the branch is either of the correct size or too small, particularly during seasonal peaks in trade.

In-store location The best method of finding out where the best position for each department, range or line is in the branch is through trial and error. By measuring the results in different locations, the optimum positions can be arrived at. Most multiples aim for a standard image for departmental positions if possible.

Some of these points have already been discussed in another part of this book but the main points on this aspect are:

MAGNETS The use of some commodities to encourage customer flow within the shop (e.g. greeting cards which are not, as is popularly thought, impulse but 'reminder' goods).

GROUPING OF RELATED ITEMS These can be of the alternative, complementary or supplementary type. There is often a brand, colour or size of a commodity in a customer's mind for any particular produce. By displaying an alternative alongside the familiar one, the customer is introduced to the breadth of range available.

Signposting can aid the customer here. Everything should be done to make merchandise easy to find from the customer's point of view. A first class example of this is in paperback merchandising where many (particularly multiple) bookshops group under publisher headings instead of under subject headings (e.g. science fiction, cookery). The prime rule is, however, to give the maximum possible exposure to known best selling lines.

Layout Fixtures should be arranged to encourage customers to circulate through the whole selling area, thus making the greatest possible use of selling space. Merchandise on open sale should be clearly viewable by the customer and if possible as much opportunity as necessary should be given to the potential customer to handle and examine the product. Obviously some more expensive or fragile items would not be treated in this way or goods open to pilferage. Again prices should be clearly marked to establish values in the customer's minds.

Reorganising branches Having discussed the basics of the retailer's merchandising effort, there is a great deal which many traders can do towards making more profitable use of their selling areas.

The key question to be asked in this context is this: is the branch securing the maximum profit from its investments? This can be checked not only by comparison with similar branches but by asking six subsidiary questions, assuming that the branch is correctly located and is of the right size for its potential sales:

1 Is the correct display space being allocated to each broad category of products?
2 Is there overstocking or understocking?
3 Is the ranging correct for the demands of the local market?
4 Are the fittings suitable?
5 Are the departments correctly positioned?
6 What promotional aids are used for various departments?

The methods of approaching answers to these questions have already been outlined in the relevant sections of this book. The great advantage which the retailer carries over the manufacturer is that new ideas, merchandise and methods can be tested quickly with speedy results gained by studying customer reactions.

COST REDUCTION

Operating costs in retail branches are continually rising and it is the responsibility of the branch manager, as outlined previously, to control these expenses as far as he is able.

There are certain fixed costs which he cannot control, e.g. rent, rates, service charges, head office and supervision expenses, delivery charges, depreciation. He has some control over wages (but not over SET and National Insurance), accommodation costs such as lighting and heating, telephone expenses and shrinkage. He may, of course, require some help in the control of his variable costs, two of the most crucial of which we now discuss.

STAFFING AND PRODUCTIVITY

The charge against branch gross profit which most often vies with accommodation costs for the largest share is, of course, wage costs. The problem of wage costs is a dual one. First the correct establishment has to be worked out for each branch and second, the productivity of that establishment must be measured. Higher productivity can be gained by incentive and bonus schemes for branch staff and management (see page 126).

Appendix Xb illustrates a simple method whereby alternative staff establishments can be worked out by studying how the time available for serving customers is actually used by assistants. The diagram takes into account the fixed work which must be done in the shop, e.g. checking stock and dressing the window. This type of work should normally be fitted in when customer flows are at their lowest, customer numbers being taken off the cash register counter. Break times are also excluded from the actual time available for serving customers. One arbitrary relationship is customer serving time, in this case 100 customers per hour giving each customer 36 seconds for actual service (from her asking for a product to the bagged item being passed over the counter to her). This ratio of average time allowed for each customer can be measured by timing a sample of customers during the serving period.

An 'activity ratio' can be worked out from this data which shows in percentage form the effective use of the available time for serving customers and can be applied usefully in counter service shops. It is obviously impossible for an activity of 100 per cent to be achieved on the part of the staff, but an activity ratio of 60–70 per cent would be acceptable in a correctly staffed branch. It will be seen from the diagram in Appendix Xb that an alternative staffing with a part timer instead of two full time assistants (including the manageress) increases the activity ratio from 46 to 56 per cent over the particular day under study, thus reducing wage costs and increasing productivity.

See Appendix XI for a checklist on expenses in retail branches.

SELF-SERVICE

Much of what has already been discussed in this chapter relies implicitly on the benefits brought about by the introduction of self-service and self-selection systems in British retail units. For detailed discussions on this slightly overexposed topic the reader is asked to consult the Bibliography.

SOURCES AND REFERENCES

1 *Costs and Competition in Retailing.* W. G. McClelland. Macmillan, 1966.
2 'British Home Stores.' K. van Musschenbroek. *Financial Times.* 25 March 1969.

8

CORPORATE IDENTITY

A deliberate attempt has occurred in recent years on the part of many firms to create and improve upon the company 'personality', or the various facets of the firm as seen and experienced by customers, suppliers, staff and members of the public. The word 'image' is in some senses a misnomer when applied to the face a company projects to the world, apart from the fact that it has become slightly debased through political and other usage. A new logo, a freshly painted fleet of vans and a stock of artistically designed stationery do not create a new corporate identity in themselves: they are merely the superficial gloss in a situation where the basic concepts of the company have to be re-examined in a planned manner. It is very possible that the creation of a new corporate identity would flow from the overhauling of the company's corporate plans as it has in the Co-operative Societies. Most of the half-dozen or so UK consultants who specialise in corporate image creation see their task as similar to that of management consultants: 'Improving the quality of life in the company, easing communications and stimulating the organisation with a fresh pride.'[1]

There are many examples to illustrate the trend towards corporate image creation which, at its best, can be a particularly potent form of goodwill advertising. Plessey in the electronics field now has had a strong image created for them by Rapier Design, while Coca-Cola has recently undergone a facelift masterminded by Lippincott and Margulies, the American corporate image consultants. This new look has been described by the consultants as 'A system in which all of the visual elements can pull together as one for the first time in the history of Coca-Cola'. The particular problem in this case was designing a brand image which would be readily identifiable in the 135 countries where the drink is advertised and where the 'sign has come to be plastered in differing shapes, scripts and colours throughout the world'.[2] A less simple problem in international marketing is posed by Unilever and its many food products where international branding has to take account of varying national tastes, customs and eating habits. British retailers with the exception of Mothercare, Burton, W. H. Smith and one or two others do not face the problem of international operations. But in common with French retailers in Britain (e.g. Pronuptia) the home grown names have been retained abroad.

Before discussing corporate identity in detail it may be interesting to discuss an article published a few years ago in the *Financial Times*. Here the creative director of a design consultancy, writing about department stores in particular, outlined the three main areas where:

> 'Many quite competently managed stores fail from a personality standpoint. First they don't know what they mean to people, or what people want from them. There is very little communication between them and their customers or potential customers . . . The second failure is lack of co-ordination. Window displays are in one idiom. In-store displays in another. The design of an interior is often unsympathetic to the merchandise. It's no good having "we've got a new personality" type advertising or design tricks in the *avant garde* boutique idiom, if you still have the same dreadful hierarchical "supervisor/assistant" performance going on in the store.'
>
> 'The third area of failure is a basic unawareness of radical changes in techniques of promotion.'

The writer of this article also hints cleverly at the psychological impact of description, viz:

> 'Strawberries, lovely strawberries—half-a-dollar, half a pound': a street market.
>
> 'Royal Sovereign strawberries—best flavour—three shillings a punnet': a high street greengrocer.
>
> 'Strawberries—compost grown, unsprayed, direct from the grower to us': a health food shop.
>
> 'Ripe Royal Sovereign strawberries from Somerset—five shillings a pound': a multiple supermarket.
>
> 'Hothouse strawberries—specially flown from Kenya—ten shillings a pound': a West End Store.

'This assumes they're all in the same condition, they actually taste pretty much the same, although there are subtle differences:

'The personality of a store is hard to analyse. What is it that makes you never dream about worrying about the quality of freshness of bacon in one store, while in another you doubt the authenticity of a national brand's date stamp?'[3]

This writer, although outlining certain truths, has imputed almost a semi-mystical quality to retail personality which depends largely on the psychological interplay between the (sometimes) complex mind of the public and the tactics by which retailers attempt to sell their goods. This chapter only attempts to describe the basic problems of creating a recognisable personality and must needs deal in the physical rather than metaphysical aspects.

In retailing, the problem of corporate identity is the face-to-face situation which the retailer experiences with the general public. It cannot be stressed too forcibly that the corporate personality of a retail firm must be one not only acceptable to the shopping public but also one which is remembered and which, at every exposure, imprints itself upon the public mind. Any weaknesses in a current corporate image should be identified, corrected and the results integrated with the rest of the company's image to form a total personality which in itself creates among the shopping public an active desire to patronise the company's branches. We now discuss the component parts of a corporate retail image. Weaknesses can be identified by market research; the best results from surveys can be gained by using professional researchers.

COMPANY NAME

An easily remembered company name is essential to the creation of a corporate identity. Allied Suppliers are currently busy changing the many names of its various subsidiary retail chains in England to Lipton. Boots, however, decided to retain the name Timothy Whites and use it for a new hardware chain, the link between the old and new chains being the concentration on this aspect of retail trading: much goodwill has undoubtedly been retained by this decision.

The name Mothercare was created by one advertising agency (while the well known 'child in a nightgown' symbol of this firm was created by another agency). Mothercare is probably the first British company actively to promote an international image as such by opening (under the same name) in Austria, Denmark, Norway, Sweden, Switzerland and West Germany. (An illustration of the Rodøvre, Denmark branch of this chain is given in Plate 1.)

Of British Home Stores: 'It took,' according to a member of the modern company, 'an American to dream up such an awful name, but we aren't thinking of changing it.' The company was founded by the

Neisner family in the late 1920's but the name now (and no pun intended) is a household word.[4]

The Dorothy Perkins chain of women's dresswear shops was named after a type of rose, while the name Tesco is an amalgam of that of Sir Jack Cohen and his former partner T. E. Stockwell.

Some of the larger groups, particularly in baking, still trade locally under the names of firms taken over; for instance RHM Bakeries Ltd (of Ranks Hovis McDougall) trades as McVittie Guest in Edinburgh, Lowman in the Southampton area and Clark's in London.

Most retail firms are named after the founder, but the success of the Birdseye brand of foods (founded by Mr Birdseye) bears out a general conclusion that a name means nothing in itself but is an 'empty vessel' which a company's marketing fills with meaning for the consumer.[5]

Nevertheless, firms continue to select image-projecting names. Some names, particularly of catering establishments, try to evoke in their prospective patrons a feeling of nostalgia or of vicarious robustness, for example the 'Buccaneer Bar' in a well known Bournemouth Hotel. Such establishments can follow the name through in decor themes, an extension of image creation which is not so open to the ordinary retailer.

Bernard Electrical, the Manchester based retailer changed its name to Loyds 2 years ago because of a change in ownership. Shop fascias were quickly altered and television advertising helped the identity change.

If there are any rules for naming retail firms they are as follows:

LENGTH

Names should not be overlong. If they are, they are generally shortened by the public (e.g. 'British Home', 'Timothy Whites'; it will be noted that Boots Ltd have dropped the 'and Taylors').

MESSAGE

If possible (and appropriate) the name should itself put over the identity which the company wishes to project, e.g. 'Mothercare'.

SIMPLENESS

The name should be easily pronounceable and unambiguous (e.g. the name Menzies, as in John Menzies, can be pronounced at least three ways). There are, conversely, a number of successful product brand names which are sometimes difficult for British people to pronounce, such as Knorr, Volkswagen and Heinz.

TYPEFACE

Many and varied are the types of lettering used in British retailing from the Boots 'signature' to the block capitals of the variety chains. The type-

K

face adopted for a corporate image should be one easily read and easily obtainable and/or producible as it is required for a large variety of uses from company stationery, through van lettering to branch fascias. The new Fine Fare group lettering has been described as a 'dateless sans-serifed typeface, invented before the war, still completely modern to look at, and therefore reliable for a good time yet to come' (see Fig. 8.1).[6]

SYMBOLS

Logos, colophons, house signs and symbols have become so popular in industry that ennui almost sets in when one tackles the subject. A few retail examples are shown in Figs. 8.1 to 8.4. Logos normally appear with the name on van sides, own brand merchandise, shopfronts, company stationery, indeed anywhere the identity of the company impinges on the public. It is the company's signature and therefore requires to be well designed and in tune with the typefaces the company uses. It should not be too ornate, a common fault with older symbols where three or four initial letters were entwined (often by a coachpainter) in a design which, if it was pretty, was often less than explicit. It is essential when a group identity is being projected that subsidiary or associate companies

Fig. 8.1

Fig. 8.2

Fig. 8.3

Fig. 8.4

carry the same style of logo. One medium sized group known to the author had, at the time of writing, no less than three different logo designs based on the same two initial letters. The symbol should not be too complex—it should be recognisable if not literally readable—and this is an added advantage for production and printing purposes. Initial letters are not necessary in a symbol: the Mothercare 'child in a nightgown' and the Dorothy Perkins rose are two well known examples.

Some groups believe that a strong colour image is important. Fine Fare, since late 1969, have adopted orange as house colour ('since it is warm, and green does not look so good with meat, and blue is cold') while the Co-op favour a blue–green.[5] There is no doubt that colour, skilfully used and applied in large flat areas (e.g. van sides) can catch the public eye. It is a pity that so many retail firms use blue or red as a colour motif. House colours, of course, should appear on all company artifacts.

BRANCHES

LOCATION AND SITING

National multiple shops must, of necessity, be sited in prime or near prime positions in shopping centres. This is not only because they require higher customer flows and must needs share in the cumulative attraction created by other multiples, but because shoppers expect them to be there. Some shopping centres are too constricted to support adequately their catchment areas and in this situation there is often great competition between multiple retailers for sites; some of the variety stores are still not represented in certain key towns purely because they have so far been unable to assemble enough land to give themselves the gross floor areas they require. This pressure on land and the higher rentals or freehold prices resulting caused independent retailers to be forced out of central areas into secondary and tertiary positions, or into suburban shopping centres. There has been some criticism of this and of the resulting situation that many shopping centres, with their parades of retail household names, have lost their identity and become similar to other centres up and down the country. This is unfortunately a simple matter of economics and appears to be accepted by the general shopping public as a convenience rather than a burden.

SIZE AND SHAPE

Many multiple retailers require shops of certain minimum sizes to allow first class presentation of their ranges with adequate circulation space round the free standing fittings. A trend towards very much larger units has been evident over the past 5 years. Both Boots Ltd and J. Sainsbury

Ltd are currently contracting for units of up to 30,000 ft² gross area and Marks and Spencer Ltd for twice this figure. Wider store frontages now allow for larger and better spaced letterings on the fascias and generally give a better impact from the street and result in a more spacious atmosphere in the store interior. Particularly in the newer shopping developments retailers are able to secure squared off units which are easier to fit and merchandise and allow the customer to see all departments at a glance.

SHOPFRONT, FITTINGS AND LAYOUT

A great deal of work has gone into the design of shopfronts and internal fittings over the past few years and much of this has been motivated by the introduction of self-service and self-selection modes of trading by many chains since 1950. The old style of window has completely disappeared from the supermarket scene and is only retained in rudimentary form in variety stores and in other multiple branches. The see-through window allows passing shoppers to see much of the shop and the goods on display from the street without having to sort mentally through the limited range of products displayed in a window. As the images of particular retailers becomes stronger shoppers know that a certain multiple will be carrying the product she requires, and so strong is the corporate personality of some shops that she does not even have to look up at the store name to identify the retailer concerned. (Some multiples do, however, have their name or logo on the handrails of branch entrance doors.) Standard construction of the window frames, doors, transom, fascia and other components of the shopfront also aid recognition. The Dorothy Perkins chain of women's dress shops discarded their cottage roof and casement image 5 or 6 years ago, and began to carry lines other than underwear. Etam, Salisbury and Wallis among multiples catering for women shoppers, have recently changed their images and this must be due partly to the influence of the boutiques.

The lettering on the fascia is probably the most important external identification that a retailer has at his disposal. Both F. W. Woolworth and Marks and Spencer have recently made changes to their lettering, making it larger and more upstanding from the fascia, but their essential style of letter presentation has not changed. Boots Ltd on the other hand, have retained their old logo, albeit in different materials since the inception of this company; no designer would dare suggest a change to Boot's logo at this date because of distinctiveness of the signature and its ready recognition from any angle. Since taking over the Timothy Whites and Taylors chain, Boots have had the former company's fascia changed, incorporating a blue and green colour edged with white, and a Greek key symbol. There are, in fact, very few of the larger multiples which have not instituted fascia design changes over the past 5 years and this has often been supported by more up-to-date in-store designs. Image, then, is not an immutable thing and its continual updating in line with modern design thinking is vital to the projection of a fresh, forward looking shop image to the public. Most of the design changes that have occurred have made the retailers concerned more identifiable to the public through the use of clearer lettering, lighter and more attractive colours so that their images have been reinforced rather than otherwise. Mothercare have, within the last 2 or 3 years, changed the colour of their fascia lettering from dark blue to white. Selim Zilkha, the chairman, believes that this gives a more positive 'quality' image to the shop exteriors. Zilkha admits, however, that the new colour is less dramatic.

The prime functions of in-store fittings (in the narrow function as product containers) is to provide effortless commodity selection by customers and to allow easy and attractive display of merchandising. Incidentally, they can also constitute another hallmark of the retailer concerned, if taken in their widest context which includes ceiling and floor treatments, lighting and other decoration. Again, careful thought has to be put into the design of the branch interior so that it is not only acceptable to the public but does project the idea of an integrated whole. The Co-op during its recent facelift was provided with new shop layouts and, these, along with many other image changes, have been circulated in a reference manual distributed throughout the organisation.

As a further bonus, the retailer is able to secure substantial discounts on the bulk orders he places for these fittings.

MAINTENANCE

REPAIRS

The maintenance of existing shop properties is often put low on budget priorities, perhaps because of the low profitability of many branches. If a branch is not worth maintaining correctly it is not worth operating. Fortunately, the Offices, Shops and Railway Premises Act and the ministrations of local health and building inspectors do keep up standards in some areas of the country but there is still a lamentable lack of proper repair work done by retail companies on many of their properties.

CLEANING

Proper care of shop properties must include the cleaning of shopfront, floors, ceiling fittings, lights and so on at appropriate intervals. Here again a clean shop can add something to the personality of a retail chain, in the eyes of a customer.

MERCHANDISE

RANGE

The depth and breadth of a retail firm's buying policy should be part of the image the firm wishes to project, as must the quality of the goods bought and sold. Harrods department store is a case in point where the merchandise sold is very much part of that firm's image. Where low quality (and consequently low priced) goods are sold the image of the firm selling them must be proportionally lowered. The range of merchandise sold in many multiples owes more to the image the company wishes to project than to local market differences.

British Home Stores have created a name for themselves in fashion accessories, lighting and lighting accessories. By building on this success, a spin-off has occurred in that as more customers come to shop at these particular departments, the more is sold in other sections of the chain's branches. This, it is generally agreed, has produced much of the BHS sales and profit success in recent years, plus the fact that prices are deliberately aimed above Woolworth but below Marks and Spencer.

QUALITY

Probably the most important aspect of image whatever the aspect discussed is that of quality and value for money. Asked if there was any way he felt he could improve his company's image Selim Zilkha, chairman of Mothercare, said that the most important way of his firm was continual attempts to improve quality. Mothercare uses the London Textile Testing House for its quality control which is already at a high level.

PRICING POLICY

Pricing structure can be a valuable adjunct to image and particularly now that retail price maintenance has virtually been abandoned. Some retailers are still adhering to manufacturers' recommended prices, though whether through lack of confidence in their own ability to increase sales is not known. Use of sales promotion devices can also affect a company image. These should be used with a particular eye on the short and long term effect such devices have on the public image of the firm. Tesco have succeeded in becoming identified with low prices; conversely J. Sainsbury has built up its image by concentrating on perishables and associating its name with high quality. There is, of course, no necessary difference between the quality and margins of

these two chains; it is just the way they have grown. While Lord Sainsbury fought the trading stamp demon, Jack Cohen (as he then was)
helped the Tesco lower price image by fighting over resale price maintenance with Cadbury, Kayser Bondor and Imperial Tobacco.

Another well publicised battle was that of the Co-operative Wholesale
Society with local societies who were pricing own brand merchandise at
or near national brand prices which was regarded by the CWS as self-
defeating. A national price policy has now been accepted by the local
Co-ops.

It is interesting to note here, before discussing own brands more fully,
that from a price point of view they derive much of their usefulness
from the competition of manufacturers' brands and if the latter are too
badly hit the main point of the exercise is lost. Product development and
research for new and improved brands depends on the profits of the
manufacturing companies.

OWN BRANDS

When retailers' own branded merchandise was first introduced the idea
behind it was to combat retail price maintenance. As resale price
maintenance was progressively abolished, own brands took on a mo-
mentum of their own until it was realised that not only did they, in
many cases, provide better margins for retailers, but they were an
important means of helping to create a corporate image. The most successful firm's using own brands for this and other purposes have been to
date J. Sainsbury and Marks and Spencer.

The drive towards profit and the need to build up a corporate image
can move in opposite directions. Tesco doubled its sales of talcum
powder in some of its stores by having 'made for Tesco by Boots'
printed on the tins. This is not to say that Tesco is unaware of the
tremendous consumer loyalty that can be built up by merchandising
own brands. The anonymous 'Delamere' (named after the road Tesco's
head office is located in) and 'Golden Ring' were changed to 'Tesco'
with, according to the company, a doubling of turnover. Woolworth,
with a galaxy of own brand names ranging from 'Household' (paint) to
'Winfield' was at the time of writing rationalising its brand names.

It is wrong to associate own brands with quality reduction, although it
is likely that an own label baked bean line might contain a slightly
thinner tomato sauce. Indeed, some suppliers ask retailers to stipulate a
cost price and then adjust the contents to fit this price. The control the
retailer has over his own brands extends from price (including margin)
to packaging, unit and outer size and marketing.

From the retailer's point of view there are certain disadvantages to
own branding: the paperwork involved in handling and the possibility
of having to sell off unsold stock costed into the selling price could pro-

duce a loss maker. This had certainly been some experience in America. Another problem which could affect the retailer indirectly is that own brand production by manufacturers can stultify their new product development.

It appears that own brands could be reaching their peak and in the US the market share held by private labels has stayed at around 25 per cent as compared with about 20 per cent at present in UK.

'A family resemblance and a distinctiveness is aimed at in order that the customer readily identifies a package as emanating from a particular firm.'[7] Much of the phenomenal Sainsbury sales growth (almost doubled in 5 years) must be attributed to the large range of own brand merchandise in the chain stores. Sainsbury's own labels had initially the look of a talented art college student's work: they were basic in design to the point of being clinical and appeared not to be selling packs at all in the sense that for instance the excellent Kellogg cornflake boxes were and are. The name 'Sainsbury' sold the product and this was quickly realised at the end of the war when 30 or 40 variously named lines were abruptly renamed.

The development of pack design in Sainsbury's is a classic case in image creation. White was chosen as a background theme for many of the earlier packs with a minimum of wording in order to present a totally different image to that projected by the national brands. As the company's own labels have grown in importance so has more colour been introduced to own brand packs.

The rationalisation of own brand packs under a general name heading (normally that of the retailer) is going on continuously and at the time of writing Woolworth and Allied Suppliers are reported to be progressing this. The Co-op have hired the American corporate identity consultants Lippincott and Margulles. More than 2000 different packs (190 brands) have been rationalised into a common form. (See Plates 2 and 3 for examples of own-brand packs.)

TICKETING

There is some controversy in supermarketing circles as to the advisability of the 'poster parades' stuck on supermarket windows. Tesco and Fine Fare are typical examples of chains which use posters for advertising cut price lines very extensively. Even the until recently staid W. H. Cullen chain in the South East have, as part of their revamp of branches into self-service units, begun to use these posters. Sainsbury, on the other hand eschew this type of promotion. Certainly, on the grounds that the typical housewife cannot take more than two or three of these posters in at one time the effort is, in a sense, self-cancelling. The only positive argument for it is that it gives an *impression* of cut pricing to the potential customer which may come to the same thing in the end. (One could argue that simple hieroglyphics or even plain fluorescent posters would create the same effect.)

Many multiples have their price tickets and labels produced in a house style with a particular typeface which is, again, linked with the fascia lettering, stationery headings, delivery van lettering and so on. Silk screen printing and machines such as the Masson Seeley have aided this aspect of corporate image creation.

DISPLAY

Standardised displays of commodities in each branch are aided by the standard fittings which multiples now order in bulk for their shops. The fact that many of these fittings are designed for self-service or self-selection improved their display possibilities in that they allow block presentation of merchandise, so that the design and packaging of articles can have the full selling effect, make fuller use of the shop's capacity for showing goods (and this includes removal of window beds). Cleaner, more attractive branches can be produced by the use of self-service fixtures which allow neat and well displayed stock to be put on show.

The carnival effect in some supermarkets, supported by balloons, in-store posters, netting, Muzak and the rest certainly produces an image or personality of sorts. Shopping for food *is* a chore to many housewives, so let her at least have the impression that she is enjoying the trip seems to be the argument here. The success of Tesco and other supermarket groups seems to bear this out, but Sainsbury (again) appear to be just as successful in Islington as they are in Purley, without the appendages.

The clutter effect in some chains' branches is heightened by the use of supplier's fittings, many of which are naturally designed purely for the display of the suppliers' own ranges. As a result of their design they do not often fit in with the total personality of the store if there has been an attempt at corporate identity creation. Apart from that, these fittings are very often placed in the store some time after opening so that they tend to take up space which was previously used for circulation. But some retailers still appear to believe that the more stock that can be crammed into a branch the more stock will be sold: 'we are not selling fresh air' is the argument. Unfortunately, some air space is required for customer circulation.

SERVICE

Labour intensive shops are more likely to be able to offer better service to customers and service is part of a shop's image. Whether a retailer considers that the benefits either in increased goodwill (securing of future profits) or higher sales are worth the extra outlay in staff wages, in delivery and so on is more a question for the independent retailer than the multiple which has in recent years attempted to substitute capital for labour by introducing new shopfittings, checkouts, wider gangways and other self-service or self-selection equipment.

STAFF

RECRUITMENT POLICY

Multiples which can afford to offer higher wages and better conditions are naturally more likely to obtain better staff. Surprisingly enough the Marks and Spencer wage bill is only 6 per cent of its turnover which speaks very highly of the productivity of its staff. In some of the smaller food shops a wage to turnover percentage of twice this is common. By attracting better staff a retail firm is not only achieving greater productivity but projecting a more congenial image to the shopping public. An assistant who is well paid is likely to take a more careful interest in her personal appearance and, if carefully selected, is likely to have a pleasanter approach to members of the public. Multiple firms who carry out training schemes are in fact making further investment in resources. The facilities which are offered staff, although not seen by the general public, do help the image of the firm to their present or prospective employees and the higher the level of staff conditions, other things being equal, the greater the degree of staff screening can take place.

As to management and supervision, most large retail firms still expect their managers and trainees to wear dark lounge suits and white shirts. Although this approach is often decried by younger retail executives, there is still a substantial body of opinion in the retail industry which supports the view that managers should appear to be even more regimented than the staff. The recent fashion for longer hair and 'trendy' clothes has been largely discounted except in the more advanced menswear shops.

Some groups have recently developed integrated advertising house styles (e.g. Fine Fare) for recruitment purposes, aimed at bringing coherence to the requirements of subsidiary companies.

CONDITIONS

British Home Stores in common with many other multiple retailers are steadily improving staff conditions. Women are being promoted to more senior positions, free meals are allowable to all staff, a share participation scheme is now in operation for management and the old bonus system in BHS (which was based on sales and profits) has given way to a straight salary. It was felt that the bonus system was unfair to some managers because of regional variations in trade over the chain. It has been argued also that a bonus system similar to that operated in

Woolworth encouraged managers to go in for unauthorised buying which, of course, cuts across any attempts at centralised stock control systems.

Marks and Spencer, apart from the well known free hair 'do's', have now made it part of their policy not to employ more than 1000 people in a single unit. It is felt that above this level there is a serious danger of up-setting the delicate balance that exists between getting maximum effort out of employees and keeping them happy at all times.

The 5-day week has become commonplace in retailing today in this country and there is a continuous upgrading in the standards of staff accommodation and services. Some of these movements are occurring through the self-interest of a few firms because they realise that to obtain and keep competent staff their wages and conditions must be at least equal to similar organisations in the retail trade, if not outside it.

It is occasionally useful to mount attitude surveys among staff to tap the morale levels. Psychological consultants such as Mackenzie Davey and personnel selection experts such as Reed have done such surveys for firms with quite startling results in some cases. The mere fact of such a survey can, of course, boost company morale, as the Hawthorne Experiments conducted by Elton Mayo have shown.

Many multiple firms now supply a standard overall in a drip-dry nylon which may have been specially designed for the firm by a famous couturier. This is an obvious method of image projection but it seems a pity that many of the larger multiples appear to use blue for female assistants uniforms. Name badges are also useful not only for image purposes but for giving staff a feeling of individuality. Most of these badges are produced at very low cost on a portable printing machine and are based on a plastic name insert.

ADVERTISING AND PUBLIC RELATIONS

ADVERTISING

Retail companies like any other business can contribute a great deal to their images by judicious advertising. Surprisingly little is done in the Press and on television, presumably because of the large amounts spent by the manufacturers of the products sold in the shops. Reliance on the manufacturers advertising must tend to diffuse a multiple's image, but by selection of merchandise the retailer can present the image it requires through the media of suppliers' packs, sales promotion ideas and so on. Some retailers, like Tesco with its *Tesco Times*, distribute free news-papers. Tesco also spend a large proportion of their advertising budget on local press advertising.

The point about advertising by retailers is that the cost per actual purchaser is so high, i.e. there is a large wastage element in retail advertising and this proportion raises the geographical spread of the advertisements. Certainly, to gain maximum coverage, a national multiple must advertise in a national newspaper and possibly a selection of provincial organs in addition. The retailer tends more to advertise through the image projected by his shops (including the product therein) and if his image is well known the only advertising necessary is of the type known as 'goodwill'. If this is the case, Press and television advertising for the well known national multiple takes on a lesser importance, except for new branch opening, refits, extensions and the like.

Many retail firms when they are advertising for staff by themselves (although less often through a consultant) include their logo and typeface in these press advertisements. Additionally, some retail company reports have recently become very readable items, with coloured illustrations and easy-to-read charts. This is probably not entirely for the stockholders' benefit.

Summarising, in some of the larger and better known multiples, the projection to the public of retail philosophies has been a substitute for advertising and Sainsbury and Marks and Spencer are prime examples of this where quality and return of cash if not satisfied have been central to this mode of trading for many years.

PUBLIC RELATIONS

Press offices of sorts have sprung up in some multiple retail head offices. Some of these are purely complaint answering services which are, of course, part of public relations, if of a somewhat negative kind. Press releases and handouts are becoming more frequent, although in some companies policy statements for public consumption still emanate directly from the board of directors; those below board level who dare to give unscreened comment to the Press can find themselves in serious trouble. A case somewhat of this nature occurred a few years ago when an ex-employee of a large privately owned retail company made certain statements about its computer in a book which the board of directors held to be untrue and sued the offender. (The present author should make it clear that during the preparation of this book he received full co-operation from the majority of the retail firms contacted.)

TRANSPORT

The finest mobile advertisement that a company can use is its transport fleet and many retail companies take advantage of this. One of the companies making use of their delivery vehicles in this way is J. Sainsbury. (See illustration, Plate 4.) Unfortunately little imagination has been shown in choice of colours and artwork in some other companies, and colours have often been dictated by the need to match colours after minor accidents and the required standard of cleanliness of company vehicles. Some fine creative work has been done for fleets outside retailing; Plessey and Brook-Green Laundry spring to mind as examples.

STATIONERY

Paper bags, wrapping paper and recently introduced plastic carrier bags are nowadays invariably overprinted with the name of the firm, a logo or a piece of advertising copy. Sainsbury's slogans 'where good food costs less' and so on are employed on the firm's carrier bags (as it is on the delivery vans, window posters and other advertising media).

The stationery used by the company for its external correspondence is often tied in with other aspects of its image, e.g. use of standard typeface, colours, layout and so on.

COMPANY SLOGANS

Many companies have adopted slogans which attempt to crystallise the ideas they believe surround the products they sell and the environment they are sold in. 'Never knowingly undersold' and 'the store of a million gifts' are particularly evocative of what the two department store chains quoted are trying to project. Occasionally a catchy phrase has been transformed into a television jingle, the Cyril Lord couplet being one example. 'Fine Fare Care' in 1969 superseded the somewhat unwieldy 'you'll always find fairness at Fine Fare' and is again evocative of what this group is attempting to achieve.

GOODWILL

The concept of goodwill which appears to be talked of more by accountants than by others is one which cannot be ignored in the context of a discussion on image. Goodwill may have little to do with the look of shops, their cleanliness or even their staff's presentation, but can still identify a retailer in the public's mind. Although perhaps more associated with independent shops, the century of trading that, for example, Sainsbury has recently completed has built up a fund of goodwill for this supermarket chain which must have added an unquantifiable amount to its turnover through the years.

HEAD OFFICE

Although few members of the shopping public are likely to come into any sort of contact with the head office of a retail firm, some do. More importantly, supplies of manufactured foods and services often have recourse to contacting head office, personally or otherwise, to secure orders. There are several aspects to this part of a company's image which are important.

SWITCHBOARD MANNERS

Nothing can so stamp a company's image, even to a casual telephone caller, than the presentation given by the operators manning the company telephone exchange. A brusque manner, slowness, impatience, the sound of a radio or even casual conversation can produce lasting effects on callers, even those with insensitive natures! On the other hand, an air of efficiency and courtesy can have precisely the opposite effect and can add stature, however apparently trivial, to a company's image.

CORRESPONDENCE

The use of 'commercialese' has been given saturation coverage in many textbooks on letter writing and there is no point in dwelling on this fortunately diminishing problem. The fact that many managers still cannot write grammatically and syntactically correct English is another matter. Training in this area and at this level is, of course, unthinkable in many firms.

RECEPTION AREAS

Foyers and interior rooms should be furnished and decorated to conservative (acceptable) but pleasant standards of taste as here, again, a lasting impression can be made on visitors. Many retail head offices are unfortunately located in old properties, not purpose built, and the continual changes in layout which occur in expanding firms in this sort of building often present sights which are less than pretty. Receptionists themselves should be pleasant, practise a 'spontaneous smile' and 'make everyone feel important'.

In conclusion, a company image should be unequivocal, consistent and create a desire in customers to shop at the chain's branches. The creation of a corporate image which takes into account all the aspects discussed above must make a contribution to company turnover and, ultimately, to profitability.

THE COST OF A CORPORATE IDENTITY

In 1970 Woolworth instituted a new corporate identity programme of major proportions which it is estimated could cost more than £500,000. Over 1140 branches, this does not appear to be too excessive a sum.

Prices charged by consultants vary. Lippincott and Margulies, an American based firm, has charged between £3000 and £30,000 an assignment and Wolff Olins reckons on about £2000 per month, depending on the man hours devoted to each client. They apparently find that British companies are prepared to pay the fees, mainly because research has shown just how vital it is to have a good and well known corporate identity.

IMPLEMENTATION

The first step towards creating a company personality is to appoint one director or senior executive to assess the problem and make recommendations. A committee may have to be set up to give full force to the views of the 'users'. Various alternative projects should be costed and recommendations made as to whether consultants should be brought in. Like corporate planning, corporate identity produces results which are unquantifiable but, as stated previously, many firms believe that investment in this sector can produce significant long term benefits.

SOURCES AND REFERENCES

1 'Company images for sale.' A. Thorncroft. *Financial Times*. 18 June 1970.
2 'Things go wavy with Coke.' P. Judge. *Financial Times*. 3 July 1970.
3 'The elusive flavour of personality.' M. Wolff. *Financial Times*. 23 May 1968.
4 'The branding of B.H.S.' Kelsey van Musschenbroek. *Management Today*. October 1970.
5 'How to name brands.' J. H. Davidson. *Management Today*. November 1970.
6 'Colour, new symbol and a promise that they care.' *The Times*. 15 October 1969.
7 *The Management of Multiple Shops*. A. J. Sainsbury. B.I.M., 1949.

BIBLIOGRAPHY

Chapter 1
Corporate Strategy. H. I. Ansoff, Penguin Books 1968.
Modern Management Methods. E. Dale and L. C. Michelon, Penguin Books 1969.
Improving Management Performance. J. Humble, B.I.M. 1965.

Chapter 3
New Ideas in Retail Management. Edited by G. Wills, Staples Press 1970.
Business in Britain. G. Turner, Penguin Books 1971.
Mergers in Modern Business. N. A. H. Stacey, Hutchinson revised edition 1970.
Regional Shopping Centres: Their Location, Planning and Design. C. S. Jones, Business Books 1969.
The Future Pattern of Shopping., N.E.D.O., H.M.S.O. 1971.

Chapter 5
Retail Trade Developments in Great Britain 1971–1972. Gower Press 1971.
People, Shops and the 70's. J. Tanburn, Lintas 1970.
Retail Site Assessment. R. K. Cox, Business Books 1968.

Chapter 6
Self Service Retailing. R. G. Towsey, Iliffe 1964.

L

Chapter 7
Budgetary Control and Cost Reduction for Retail Companies. D. T. Welch, Macdonald and Evans 1969.
Costs and Competition in Retailing. W. G. McClelland, Macmillan 1966.
Retail Merchandising. R. D. Driscoll, Pitman 1965.
Modern Merchandising. R. G. Towsey, Iliffe 1970.
Retail Business Administration. W. J. Philpott, Pitman 1963.

Chapter 8
A Management Guide to Corporate Identity. Edited by J. E. Blake. Council of Industrial Design. 1971

The above constitutes a basic reading list to augment each chapter content.

APPENDIX I

The Town and Country Planning Act, 1968: brief summary of provisions

Although, even now, the Town and Country Planning Act of 1962 remains the principal planning Act, the 1968 Act makes many radical changes. When it was passed on 25 October 1968, however, considerable portions of the Act were left to be introduced on a piecemeal basis by means of Orders to be made. Over the succeeding months various Orders have thus appeared so that at the time of writing—late March 1969—virtually all of the provisions of the Act other than the substantive provisions as to development plans in Part I and the provisions dependent upon them will be in force by 1 May 1969. Part I of the Act, however, will be brought into force at different future times for different places; this is to ensure that the valuable new powers of planning control therein contained will only be conferred upon those local planning authorities which, in the Minister's opinion, are ready and able to administer them responsibly.

Firstly, there is a complete re-styling of the development plan procedure. The existing obligation to carry out a re-survey of the local planning authority's area every five years has been removed. Instead the authority *may*, if they so wish, institute a fresh survey of their area at any time and *must* institute one if the Minister directs them so to do. The use of the word 'institute' is deliberate for it enables a local authority to call in outside help to undertake the necessary survey: they no longer have to 'carry out' the whole of the work themselves. Having made a survey, the authority prepares and forwards to the Minister a report of such survey together with a 'structure plan' for their area. Now a 'structure plan' is, in effect, a statement of general policy indicating trends and illustrating a broad, basic pattern for the area's future development. Although there will be diagrams and descriptive matter there will be no map as such. Thus it will be quite impossible to identify precisely the effect on a particular property that structure plan proposals may have; this is left to local plan.

Now a 'local plan' is prepared by the local planning authority by reference to the overriding structure plan. It will consist of a map and a written statement setting out in such detail as the local planning authority think fit their proposals for that part of the structure plan area to which the local plan relates. The form and content of local plans will be covered by regulations and thus such plans will be the ones to which the private individual will turn to ascertain precisely the effect of the authority's proposals on his own particular property.

Returning briefly to the structure plan, however, it should be mentioned that such a plan must indicate any part of the local planning authority's area which they have selected for comprehensive treatment (and, impliedly, at an early date), in accordance with a local plan to be prepared. An area so indicated in the structure plan is an 'action area' and thus the subsequent local plan for the same area becomes an 'action area plan'. This will certainly be one of the most important of local plans and can be expected to deal with such problems as outmoded town centres, etc. Action area plans will come with different degrees of detail.

If this was all, one might say that the 1968 Act proposes two plans instead of one but there is a much more important difference. A development plan under the 1947–62 Acts had to be approved by the Minister before it could come into operation. There was an opportunity to object to the contents of the plan and such an objection would have been dealt with by the Minister. A structure plan (which it will be recalled deals in broad terms), still affords a similar protection, but a local plan (which is the one most landowners will be interested in), is to be approved and brought into operation by the local planning authority without, normally, any intervention by the Minister. The word 'normally' is used because the Minister retains powers of 'call in'. Thus, objections to a local plan must be sent to the local authority who actually prepared it and not to the Minister. Regulations will cover this new aspect.

Finally, in this respect it should be noted that the new development plan arrangements are modified in their application to Greater London.

Secondly, there is a change in the planning appeals procedure. Planning appeals have proved an increasing burden to the Ministry of

Housing and Local Government; in 1967 over 60 per cent of all appeals related to relatively minor forms of development which did not raise issues of Ministerial policy. Thus, as in the overwhelming number of cases (about 97·5 per cent), the Minister accepted his own inspector's recommendations, it clearly followed that delegation of responsibility for actually deciding appeals of a non-policy raising nature could be made. The 1968 Act provides for this delegation and regulations will govern the nature of those appeals which may be directly decided by an inspector. The Minister, however, retains powers to restore to himself the responsibility of determining any particular appeal.

Thirdly, the enforcement of planning control attracts new provisions. In this connection it will be remembered that, hitherto, if unauthorised development could continue in being for four years without attracting an enforcement notice it then automatically became 'legal' by reason of the fact that no enforcement notice could thereafter be served in respect of such development. This still remains the case under the new act for 'operations' or a change of use of any building to use as a single dwelling house. For all other changes of use in breach of planning control a local planning authority will be able to serve an enforcement notice where it appears to them that such a breach has occurred after the end of 1963.

It will at once be appreciated that, as there is no time limit, the passage of years could mean that at some distant date the person having the benefit of an allegedly unauthorised use may have great difficulty in proving the use was, in fact, established at a time which frees it from challenge, e.g. before the end of 1963. There is thus provision in the 1968 Act to apply to a local planning authority for a certificate indicating a particular use of land as an established use.

Enforcement notices must be served on the owner and the occupier of the 'land' to which it relates and optionally upon any other person who, in the opinion of the local planning authority, possesses an interest in the land which is materially affected by the notice. Additionally, and an entirely new provision, the local planning authority may serve at the same time as the enforcement notice, or at any time thereafter but before the enforcement notice takes effect, a *stop notice*. This notice, which does not apply to change of use cases (except refuse or waste material deposits) but only to development operations, means exactly what its name implies. It prohibits any person on whom it is served from carrying out, or continuing, the operations alleged to be in breach of planning control or so closely associated with such operations as to constitute substantially the same operations. The reasoning behind the stop notice is the necessity to prevent the delaying action, previously adopted by offenders, whereby determination of an appeal against an enforcement notice could be unduly prolonged with obvious benefit to the appellants. On the other hand provision is now made for the payment of compensation, in certain specified cases relating basically to successful opposition to an enforcement notice, where loss or damage directly attributable to a stop notice is occasioned.

Fourthly, the new Act does not contain any provision as to the designation of land in development plans as subject to compulsory acquisition. Thus, although such designation may exist in development plans by virtue of the 1962 Act, as soon as the new structure and local plan procedure comes into force in any particular area such designation will cease to have effect. Consequently, provisions authorising the compulsory purchase of land by local authorities and certain Ministers are now enacted to link compulsory purchase procedure to the new development plan procedure. There are, however, additional provisions relating to compulsory purchase of importance. For example, under the 1968 Act an acquiring authority having obtained a compulsory purchase order may execute a 'general vesting declaration' vesting the land, covered by the operative compulsory purchase order, in themselves as from the end of such period as may be specified in the declaration. Such a period must not be less than 28 days from the date on which the service of the relevant notices required by Schedule 3 of the 1968 Act is completed.

Further examples relate to the vexed question of planning 'blight'. The new development plans procedure leads to four new grounds (two of which, in effect, are replacement grounds), on which a purchase notice deriving from blight may be served on a local authority. Such an authority, however, is itself granted a new ground whereby it may counter a 'blight' purchase notice. This provides that given stated circumstances the local authority shall not be obliged to purchase the land so blighted if they do not propose to acquire the land in the exercise of their compulsory powers for a period of fifteen years or more. Another new provision allows for the payment of compensation for severance and disturbance in 'blight' purchase notice acquisition. Formerly this was not so and therefore was a financial deterrent to would be 'claimants'.

Fifthly, there are new proposals relating to the preservation of buildings of special architectural or historical interest. Previously, it will be recalled, such buildings could be protected if they were made subject to a building preservation order; their inclusion only in a list of buildings of special architectural or historical interest under Section 32 of the Act of 1962 did not confer a similar measure of protection. Under the 1968 Act, however, the listing of a building will give a full measure of protection: indeed so much so that Building Preservation Orders are no more. On the 1 January 1969 any building then subject to a Building Preservation Order but not a listed building under the 1962 Act became a listed building under the 1968 Act. It is now an offence, punishable by imprisonment or fine, or both, to demolish, alter or extend a listed building without a specific written grant of consent from the local planning authority or the Minister. Such a consent is to be known as a listed building consent and may be granted with or without conditions: it can be the subject of an appeal to the Minister. If a listed building consent is refused or, in the opinion of the owner of the building, the conditions attached to the consent are so onerous that in either event the listed building in its existing state has become incapable of reasonable beneficial use he may serve a 'listed building purchase notice' requiring the appropriate local authority to purchase the listed building. Provision is also made for local authorities to acquire compulsorily any listed building which is not being properly 'preserved'. The power cannot, however, be exercised unless at least two months previously the local authority has served on the owner of the building, and not withdrawn, a repairs notice specifying the works which they consider reasonably necessary for the proper preservation of the building and explaining the effect of the relevant provisions of the 1968 Act.

If a listed building is compulsorily acquired then the compensation will, unless the building has been deliberately left to get derelict, be based on the assumption that listed building consent would have been granted for any works of alteration or extension not subject to a prior refusal or, indeed, for its demolition. Where the building has been allowed to become derelict, however, for the purpose of justifying its demolition and the development or redevelopment of the site or any adjoining site the local authority may include in the compulsory purchase order submitted to the Minister an application that he direct minimum compensation be payable. Such compensation excludes, in effect, all development potential whether by way of redevelopment or by way of alteration or extension.

Sixthly, and of some significance, are the proposals to place limitations on the duration of planning permissions both as to those granted in the past and those in the future. As to past permissions, only those where development had not begun before the 1 January 1968 are affected. Outlined permissions already granted will lapse on the 1 April 1972 if approval of details has not by then been applied for: detailed permissions already granted will lapse on 1 April 1974 if development has not then begun.

As to the future permissions the local planning authority have discretion to shorten or lengthen the normal limitations which are:

1 Outline permission will lapse three years from the date of the permission if approval of details have not by then been applied for, or two years after final approval of details if work has not then begun.

2 Detailed permissions will lapse five years from the date of the permission if development has not by then begun.

Development is deemed to have 'begun' on the earliest date on which a 'specified operation' as defined in the Land Commission Act, 1967 begins to be carried out. If, however, development has 'begun' but not been completed within the time limitations applicable to the permission and the local authority are of the opinion that the development will not be completed within a reasonable period they may serve a 'completion notice' stating that the permission will cease to have effect at the end of such a period as is specified in the notice. This period must not be less than twelve months after the notice takes effect.

Finally, there may be summarised various other changes which the Act of 1968 and Orders, etc. made thereunder bring about:

1 The period under which an appeal can be made to the Minister against a planning application decision is increased from one month to six months.

2 Planning registers kept by planning authorities are to be in two parts: the first giving full details (include availability of plans) of applications still outstanding, the second giving a full record of decisions.

3 If a local planning authority wish to do so they may delegate to any officer of the authority the function of determining planning applications of a kind set out in the Act.

4 The carrying-out of works for the alteration of a building by providing additional space *below* ground level is to rank as development requiring planning permission.

5 The Minister may constitute a planning Inquiry Commission to enquire into and report on particular matters where there are considerations of national or regional importance, *or* the technical or scientific aspects of the proposed development are of so unfamiliar a character as to jeopardise a proper determination of that question unless there is a special inquiry for the purpose.

The above commentary is not regarded by its authors as being comprehensive, but was intended as a simple guide to the main provisions of the Act.

APPENDIX II
New shop pre-planning checklist

1 Detail received from agent.
2 Detail checked to see if site is:
    (*a*) In development area.
    (*b*) In acceptable pitch and location.
    (*c*) Of correct size and frontage.
    (*d*) At acceptable rent.
3 If above criteria fulfilled:
    (*a*) Agent told of interest.
    (*b*) Architect drawn plans requested.
4 Site assessor visits site and checks:
    (*a*) Agent's detail.
    (*b*) Competition.
    (*c*) Pedestrian flows.
    (*d*) Local planning.
5 If site acceptable site assessor:
    (*a*) Reports briefly to development manager.
    (*b*) Writes assessment report.
6 Agent contacted and told that property is acceptable subject to contract and survey.
7 Survey carried out.
8 Surveyor reports to estates manager.
9 Estates department produces estimates for fitting and building costs.

10 Estates department studies lease.
11 Contracts exchanged if no legal or structural difficulties.
12 Date of entry and rent free period (if any) established.
13 Shop planner produces layout.
14 Layout agreed.
15 Estates ask for necessary tenders.
16 Tenders and work programme agreed.
17 Final capital costs agreed and entered in budget.
18 Refined sales estimates entered in revenue budget.
19 Project goes to local planning authority.
20 All appropriate staff informed of project.
21 Establishment calculated.
22 Initial stock selection made by appropriate merchandise controllers.
23 Opening promotions agreed.
24 Personnel begins discussions for branch management.

Shop opening schedule itself commences.

APPENDIX III

Checklist for shop opening

A:	Advertising	MC:	Merchandise Controller
AC:	Accountants	P:	Personnel Department
AM:	Area Manager	RDM:	Retail Development
BOM:	Branch Opening Manager		Manager
E:	Estates Department	RPO:	Regional Personnel Officer
GM:	General Manager	ST:	Staff Trainers
M:	Branch Manager		

Date: Shop:

Time before opening	Action required	Person(s) responsible	Checking column and any notes of incomplete or postponed jobs
16 weeks	Fittings for shop to be ordered	E	
12 weeks	Any minor layout alterations finalised	E	
	Electricity, gas and water supplies checked	E	
11 weeks	Wet trades begin (if necessary)	E	
	Advertising board up	E	
	Manager's house to be found (if necessary)	E	

Appendix III

Date: Shop:

Time before opening	Action required	Person(s) responsible	Checking column and any notes of incomplete or postponed jobs
10 weeks	Vacuum cleaners ordered (if shop to be carpeted)	E	
	Fire extinguishers ordered	E	
	Safe ordered	E	
	Selection of opening stock begins	MC	
	Cash registers and till rolls ordered	E	
	Final opening date announced and circulated	RDM	
	Burglar alarm ordered	E	
9 weeks	Application for telephone and directory entry	E	
	Wet trades finish	E	
	Shell ready for fitting	E	
	Local Ministry of Employment and Productivity and Youth Employment Services contacted on staff position and local rates of pay	RPO	
	Newspaper space for staff recruitment and opening promotion advertisements booked	A	
	Shop code number supplied by accountants or EDP	AC	
	'Goods for use' pack and fire notices ordered	BOM	
	Departmental and promotion signs ordered	BOM	
	Manager selected	P	
8 weeks	Shop fitting begins	E	

Date: Shop:

Time before opening	*Action required*	*Person(s) responsible*	*Checking column and any notes of incomplete or postponed jobs*
8 weeks	Branch stationery ordered from printing department	BOM	
	Opening window bills and promotional material prepared and ordered	BOM	
	Stock orders checked. Promotion lines checked	MC BOM	
7 weeks	Electricity meters, etc. signed for	E	
	Stock orders sent to suppliers with special promotional orders	MC	
6 weeks	Burglar alarm fitted	E	
	Staff advertisements prepared for press. Liaison with advertising department	P	
	Contracts exchanged for manager's house	E	
5 weeks	Shop fitting checked on site	E BOM	
	Staff advertisements in local newspaper	A	
	Staff window bills up	AM	
4 weeks	Manager takes up duties	AM	
	Vacuum cleaners in branch	E	
	Staff trainers informed of staff starting day	RPO	
	Regular visits by BOM and occasional visits by RDM from this week	BOM RDM	
	Merchandisers advised if and when merchandising assistance required	BOM	

Date: Shop:

Time before opening	Action required	Person(s) responsible	Checking column and any notes of incomplete or postponed jobs
4 weeks	Local cleaning services arranged	M	
	Staff interviewing commences	RPO	
	Head office/area help in stocking shop finalised	GM BOM	
	Arrival in branch of departmental and promotional signs/tickets plus promotion cards	BOM	
3 weeks	Handover: shopfitting complete	RDM E	
	GPO telephone installed	E	
	Transfer account with local bank. Night safe wallets and manager's signature checked	M	
	Opening window bills and promotion bills up	M	
	Second staff interviews	RPO	
	Staff overall sizes checked	BOM	
	Rates of pay to hand	RPO	
	Selected staff notified by first class mail	RPO	
12 days	Finalising of advertising in local press	A BOM	
	Police informed of shop manager's address	M	
	Local authority contacted to collect rubbish on opening day minus one	M	
	Wages department informed of cash requirements for staff payment	M	

Date: Shop:

Time before opening	Action required	Person(s) responsible	Checking column and any notes of incomplete or postponed jobs
12 days	Telephone checked	M	
	Head office notify all persons concerned of address, number of shop and telephone number	RDM	
	Post box arranged by head office	RDM	
11 days	Transport advised of date and time of first deliveries (if appropriate)	BOM	
	Staffroom furniture and first aid cabinet ordered	M	
10 days	Staff overalls ready	BOM	
	Shops Act notices up	BOM	
	Staffroom furniture in restroom (also towels and soap in cloakroom)	BOM	
	First aid cabinet in	BOM	
	Dymo machine available and name badges produced	BOM	
9 days	Price lists, markers available	BOM	
	Key control: back door should be secured	M	
	National Insurance cards and P45's from staff	M	
	Layout plan pinned up	BOM	
	Shelves taped with space allocation marked in ballpoint pen	BOM	
	If frosty, water turned off at mains and taps, etc. Continued hereafter	M	
	Part staff in today	M	

Date: Shop:

Time before opening	Action required	Person(s) responsible	Checking column and any notes of incomplete or postponed jobs
9 days	Shopfitting checked	BOM	
	Fixtures cleaned and sizes adjusted	staff	
	Suitable areas prepared for stock in stockroom	staff	
	Work prepared for staff explained and demonstrated	M	
	Security light on in the shop	M	
8 days	'Goods for use' pack delivered	BOM	
	Arrival of cash registers checked. Progressed each day until delivered	BOM	
	Security organisation informed of cash register numbers	M	
	Shelves to be fitted after checking shelf heights. One experienced merchandiser with one staff or inexperienced helper	staff M	
	Cash register till rolls should have arrived	BOM	
7 days	Fire extinguishers should be installed	BOM	
	Fire exit notices put up	BOM	
	Floor cigarette bins to hand	BOM	
	Shelf filling continued	staff	
	Waste bins distributed	staff	
6 days	In-store supervision continued and allocations adjusted	BOM	
	Teams switched so that they all get to know one another	M	

Date: Shop:

Time before opening	Action required	Person(s) responsible	Checking column and any notes of incomplete or postponed jobs
6 days	Invoices checked to date for price errors	BOM	
	Work diaried continuously	M	
	Windows and display cases cleaned inside and out	staff	
5 days	Deliveries checked and booked as they arrive	M	
	Window and display cases planned	BOM	
	Progress checked and last four days before opening planned	BOM	
	Wages book compiled and sent to computer department to ensure wages are correct for following week	M	
	List checked over to see if anything has been missed	BOM	
	Shelf filling proceeds	staff	
	Shelf filling terminated two hours before leaving and floor cleared completely, including stockroom, ready for cleaners (cleaners in at weekend)	staff	
4 days	Full staff in today. Induction training. Shown and explained branch working and layout	ST M	
	New staff NHI cards and P45's collected	M	
	Staff checked with throughout the day. Explanation and demonstration	BOM M	
	Programme prepared for tomorrow	BOM	

M

Date: Shop:

Time before opening	Action required	Person(s) responsible	Checking column and any notes of incomplete or postponed jobs
4 days	Completion of cleaning checked	M	
	Check that head office sent till floats	BOM	
	Gaps in displays checked and adjustments made	BOM	
3 and/or 2 days	Staff continue merchandising. BOM to inspect	staff	
3 and/or 2 days	Programme prepared for opening day minus one	BOM	
1 day	Wrapping paper at cash points	staff	
	Branch cleaned throughout	staff	
	Store and stockroom cleared when work completed	staff	
	Rubbish at back should be cleared by local council	BOM	
	Floats arrive from head office	BOM	
	Floats prepared and stored ready for tomorrow	BOM	
	Staff schedule for tomorrow prepared. Lunch rota worked out	M	
	Checklist for tomorrow completed	BOM	
Opening day	Checklist at hand and worked from section by section	BOM	
	Staff called together and thanked for their cooperation in preparing the branch	M	
	Staff duties outlined and reminders given of security procedure on shop lifting, prices, use of till, etc.	M	

Date: Shop:

Time before opening	Action required	Person(s) responsible	Checking column and any notes of incomplete or postponed jobs
Opening day	Team reminded of their positions when branch opens and their lunch rota arrangements	M	
	Floats in register	M	
	Clean overalls for all staff	M	
	Ribbon 'in' doors	M	
	Staff in position	M	
	SHOP OPENS		

APPENDIX IV

Profitability of a multiples' branches by sales bands

TABLE 1   Sales band £10,000–£20,000 p.a.

Profit/loss p.a. (£)	Total number of shops	Shops producing over 5% net profit
2,000 and over	–	–
1,500–2,000	1	1
1,000–1,500	–	–
500–1,000	1	–
B/E–500	1	–
Loss up to (500)	2	–
(500)–(1,000)	3	–
(1,000)–(1,500)	–	–
(1,500) and over	1	–
TOTALS	9	1

TABLE 2   Sales band £20,000–£30,000 p.a.

Profit/loss p.a. (£)	Total number of shops	Shops producing over 5% net profit
2,000 and over	—	–
1,500–2,000	2	2
1,000–1,500	8	5
500–1,000	6	–
B/E–500	6	–
Loss up to (500)	2	–
(500)–(1,000)	8	–
(1,000)–(1,500)	3	–
(1,500) and over	3	–
TOTALS	38	7

TABLE 3   Sales band £30,000–£40,000 p.a.

Profit/loss p.a. (£)	Total number of shops	Shops producing over 5% net profit
2,000 and over	12	12
1,500–2,000	5	2
1,000–1,500	5	—
500–1,000	4	—
B/E–500	5	—
Loss up to (500)	1	—
(500)–(1,000)	1	—
(1,000)–(1,500)	—	—
(1,500) and over	4	—
TOTALS	37	14

TABLE 4   Sales band £40,000–£50,000 p.a.

Profit/loss p.a. (£)	*Total number of shops*	*Shops producing over 5% net profit*
2,000 and over	18	18
1,500–2,000	1	—
1,000–1,500	2	—
500–1,000	2	—
B/E–500	1	—
Loss up to (500)	1	—
(500)–(1,000)	—	—
(1,000)–(1,500)	—	—
(1,500) and over	1	—
TOTALS	26	18

TABLE 5   Sales band £50,000–£100,000

	£50,000–£60,000	£60,000–£70,000	£70,000–£80,000	£80,000–£90,000	£90,000–£100,000
Shops producing 5% net profit	6	5	5	4	4
Shops producing profit from break-even to 5%	3	3	2	–	–
Shops making loss	1	–	1	–	–
TOTALS	10	8	8	4	4

Note: B/E = break-even point

APPENDIX V

Four multiples' coverage in London

BHS	Mothercare	J. Menzies	W. H. Smith
		Acton (Elm Park)	
			Baker St
	Barnet	Barnet	Barnet
	Barking		
	Bexleyheath		
			Beckenham
		Blackheath	
		Bond Street	
Brixton	Brixton		
	Bromley		Bromley
			Brompton Rd
		Cheapside	Cheapside
			Cheswick
	Clapham Jct.		
		Coulsdon	
			Crouch End
	Croydon		Croydon
		Dorset Square	
			Ealing
			Earls Court

BHS	Mothercare	J. Menzies	W. H. Smith
East Ham	East Ham		East Ham
		East Sheen	
		Edgware	Edgware
	Edmonton		
			Elephant & Castle
		Ewell	
		Finchley (Ballards Lane)	Finchley
			Forest Hill
			Gants Hill
		Golders Green	Golders Green
Hackney			
			Hampstead
	Harrow		
			Hatch End
			Hendon
	Holloway		
Hounslow	Hounslow		
Ilford	Ilford		Ilford
			Kensington
			Kenton
Kilburn	Kilburn		Kilburn
Kingston	Kingston		Kingston
			Kingsway
Lewisham	Lewisham		
Leytonstone			
			London Wall
			Mill Hill
			Museum Street
			Muswell Hill
			Notting Hill Gate
		Oakwood	
		Old Broad St	
	Orpington		Orpington
Oxford St	Oxford St		
		Palmers Green	Palmers Green
Peckham	Peckham		
		Perivale	
			Purley

BHS	Mothercare	J. Menzies	W. H. Smith
Putney			Putney
			Richmond
Romford	Romford		Romford
			Ruislip
			Sloane Square
		Sloane Street	Sloane Street
		South Kensington	
			S. Hampstead
		Strand	
Sutton	Sutton	Sutton	Sutton
		Sydenham	
			Temple Fortune
Tooting	Tooting		
	Uxbridge		Uxbridge
			Wallington
Walthamstow	Walthamstow	Walthamstow	Walthamstow
			Walton-on-Thames
		Wealdstone	
Wembley		Wembley	Wembley
West Ealing	West Ealing		
			West Wickham
			Willesden Green
		Wimbledon	
Wood Green	Wood Green		
Woolwich	Woolwich		

APPENDIX VI

Mothercare expansion list (UK): 1970

Branches are required in the towns listed below. Re-sites sought in towns in italics. We require best positions, or very prominent off-position units. Minimum frontage 27 feet—2,500 square feet trading, plus 2,200 square feet stock and staff room. Rear access absolutely necessary. Please do not offer small units, unless there is a possibility of acquiring the property next door. We will purchase freeholds outright. We will pay agent's fees where appropriate. Details of any properties to be sent in writing to:

Barney Goodman, Mothercare Ltd., Cherry Tree Road, Watford, Herts.

All offers acknowledged.

England and Wales

Aldershot	Canterbury	Deptford	Great
Ashford (Kent)	Carlisle	*Derby*	Yarmouth
	Chelmsford	Dewsbury	Guildford
Bath	Cheltenham		
Bedford	Chichester	*East Ham*	Halifax
Belfast	Corby New	Enfield	Harlow
Bolton	Town	Epsom	Hemel
Brent Cross	Crawley		Hempstead
Brentwood		Folkestone	High Wycombe
Brixton	Dalston	Gravesend	
Cambridge	Dartford	Grays	Kidderminster

174

King's Lynn	Newbury	St. Helens	Torquay
Kingston		*Sheffield*	
	Oxford	*Slough*	Warrington
Lancaster		Southport	Wembley
Leamington		Staines	West
Spa	Peckham	Stratford E.	Bromwich
Leeds	Putney	Stockton-on-	Wigan
Lewisham		Tees	Worthing
Macclesfield	Reading	Stourbridge	Wrexham
	Richmond	Swansea	
Newcastle on	Rochdale		Yeovil
Tyne	Rotherham	*Tooting*	

Scotland

Ayr	Falkirk	Inverness	Paisley
			Perth
Dumfries	Greenock	Kirkcaldy	
Dundee			Stirling

Mothercare shops are presently open and trading in the following towns
United Kingdom

Ashton-under-	Burton-on-	Edinburgh	Kingston
Lyne	Trent	Edmonton	
Aylesbury		Exeter	Leeds
	Cambridge		(Briggate)
Barking	Cardiff	Glasgow	Leeds
Barnet	Chatham	Gloucester	(Merrion)
Barnsley	Chester	Guildford	Leicester
Basildon	Clapham		Letchworth
Basingstoke	Colchester	Hamilton	Lewisham
Bedford	Coventry	Hanley	Lincoln
Bexleyheath	Crewe	Harrow	Llandudno
Blackburn	Croydon	Harrogate	Luton
Blackpool	Cwmbran	Hereford	
Bournemouth		Holloway	Maidstone
Bradford	Darlington	Hounslow	Manchester
Brighton	Derby	Huddersfield	Margate
Bristol	Doncaster	Hull	Middlesbrough
Brixton			
Bromley	Ealing West	Ilford	Newport
Bull Ring	Eastbourne	Ipswich	Northampton
Burnley	East Ham	Kilmarnock	Norwich

Nottingham	Pontypridd	Southampton	Wakefield
Nuneaton	Portsmouth	Southend	Walsall
	Preston	South Shields	Walthamstow
Oldham		Stafford	Watford
Orpington	Romford	Stevenage	Wolver-
Oxford		Stockport	hampton
Oxford St	St. Albans	Stretford	Wood Green
	Salisbury	Sunderland	Woolwich
Peckham	Sheffield	Sutton	Worksop
Perry Barr	Shrewsbury	Swindon	
Plymouth	Slough		York
Poole	Solihull	Tooting	

Opening 1970

Altringham	Erdington	Llanelli	Peterborough
		Liverpool	
Bootle	Hartlepool		Scunthorpe
		Merthyr Tydfil	
Dunfermline	Kilburn		Worcester

Opening 1971

Aberdeen	Bromsgrove	Dudley	Grimsby

Opening 1972

Birkenhead

Customer survey questionnaire

CLASSIFICATION DETAILS

Name of interviewer   ———————————————
Interview number   ———————————————
Date   ———————————————
Shop   ———————————————
Time taken to interview   ———————————————
Name of respondent   ———————————————
Address   ———————————————
                             ———————————————
                             ———————————————
                             ———————————————

Head of Household's Occupation———————————————

Age Group 16–24
          25–40
          40 +

Introduction:

We are doing a survey on ——— shops. Will you help us please?

Q1 Before entering the shop had you ever heard of ———?

                         Yes......
                         No......

If yes:—Is this your first visit?

Yes......
No......

If no:—Do you come:—Often   ......
Occasionally......
Rarely   ......

Q2 Did you come in with a specific purchase in mind?

Yes......
No......

If yes:—A. What? ....
B. Did you find the department you required
(i) Easily?
(ii) With some difficulty?

Q3 Did you buy anything that you did not intend buying when you entered the shop?
If so did you (a) buy the item(s) on your own impulse
or (b) was the item(s) suggested to you by an assistant

Q4 Here is a short list of articles which ———— sell. Could you tell me the ones which you did not know we had until entering the shop?

Q5 Did the shop have a wide enough variety of goods for your needs?

Yes......
No......

If no:—What do you think could be improved upon?
(Customer's own words)

....
....

Q6 How likely are you to visit ———— in the future?

Definitely going to......
Very likely   ......
Quite likely   ......
Not very likely   ......
Definitely not   ......

Why is that? ....

Q7 What do you particularly like about ————?
....

Q8 What do you particularly dislike about ————?
....

Q9 Where might you shop for these commodities (show list) other than ————?
....

Retail site investigation (Competition Checklist)

Town/Shopping Centre: _____

(1) Direct competition   Approximate sales area   m^2

Address:

Depts/categories (tick)	A	B	C	D	E	F

	Refit within 3 years	Refit within 10 years	Over 10 years
Shop front			
Fittings			

(2) Associated competition

Category/ Department	Name and address (Mark on sketch plan)	Remarks
A		
B		
C		
D		
E		
F		

Number of shops in the trade in shopping centre:

Prime multiple positions in centre
      (Street numbers and names, e.g. Marks & Spencer)

(1)
(2)
(3)
(4)

APPENDIX IX

Property budget form, 1971–72

Region ....   Area ....

Super-market	Building work	Complete refit	Part* refit	Internal decoration	External decoration	Lighting	Misc.
Self-service shop							
Manager's Accommodation							

* Please list units etc. required.

Capital Project Appraisal

Year	Projected branch X		Projected branch Y	
	Net cash income £	Capital outlay £	Net cash income £	Capital outlay £
0	(1,000)	5,000 at yr. 0	800	4,000 at yr. 0
1	2,400		800	
2	2,400		800	
3	2,400		1,600	
4	3,200		1,600	
5	3,200		1,600	
6	3,200		2,400	
7	4,000	1,500 at yr. 7	2,400	
8	4,000		2,400	
9	4,000		3,200	
10	4,400		3,200	
11	4,400		3,200	3,500 at yr. 11
12	4,400		4,000	
13	4,000		4,000	
14	4,000	2,000 at yr. 14	4,000	
15	4,000		4,000	
16	3,200		4,000	
17	3,200		4,000	
18	3,200		4,000	
19	3,200		4,000	
20	3,200		4,000	
Totals:	69,000	8,500	60,000	7,500

Further methods of appraising capital projects, particularly alternative investments, are based on a net cash income table over the life of the project (above). Either the total cash income can be matched with the total capital outlay:

$$\text{e.g.} \quad \frac{\text{Total cash income} - \text{Total capital outlay}}{\text{Total capital outlay}} \times \frac{100}{1}$$

or an average net income over project life can be used

$$\text{e.g.} \quad \frac{\text{Average annual net income}}{\text{Total capital outlay}} \times \frac{100}{1}$$

Further sophistication can be built in by the use of discounted cash flow tables which show the present values of the annual net cash incomes if they were invested on receipt at compound rates of interest.

N

APPENDIX Xb

Table showing alternative staffing in counter service food shop over one day

CASE 1

A.M. P.M.

Time	8.30	9.30	10.30	11.30	12.30	1.30	2.30	3.30	4.30	Total
A = Time available (mins)	120	105	105	90	60	90	105	105	120	900 min
B = Fixed work	90	Nil	45	30	Nil	15	15	Nil	60	255 ,,
C = Serving time	30	105	60	60	60	75	90	105	60	645 ,,
D = Number of customers per hour	25	28	32	35	31	32	27	36	21	267 ,,
E = Work to 60 mins/100 customers	15	17	19	21	19	19	16	22	13	161 ,,
F = %$\frac{B+E}{A}$ = Activity%	88	16	61	57	32	38	30	21	61	46%

	Duty total	Breaks/meals	Work Hours
Assistant (1)	9	1½	7½
Assistant (2)	9	1½	7½
	18	3	15

CASE 2

A.M. P.M.

Time	8.30	9.30	10.30	11.30	12.30	1.30	2.30	3.30	4.30	Total
A = Time available (mins)	120	90	120	75	90	90	45	60	60	750 min
B = Fixed time	90	Nil	30	Nil	15	30	Nil	30	60	255 ,,
C = Serving time	30	90	90	75	75	60	45	30	Nil	495 ,,
D = Customers	25	28	32	35	31	32	27	36	21	267 ,,
E = Work to 60 mins/100 customers	15	17	19	21	19	19	16	22	13	161 ,,
F = %$\frac{B+E}{A}$ = Activity%	88	19	41	28	38	55	36	87	122	56%

	Duty total	Breaks/meals	Work Hours
Assistant (1)	9	1½	7½
Assistant (2)	5½	½	5
	14½	2	12½

NOTES The 'time available' excludes break times. 'Fixed work' refers to window dressing, checking of deliveries, etc.
The lower set of figures shows the situation after dispensing with a second assistant during the afternoon.
E relationship allows a serving time per customer of 36 seconds.

APPENDIX XI
Checklist of retail expenses

The following is not offered as an exhaustive list of questions for retail management but rather as a mind-jogger to create lateral trains of thought on the question of retail expenses. See chapter 7.

COST OF GOODS

Do mark-ups add up to an acceptable gross margin in total?

Can they be improved? By negotiating better discounts, by placing larger orders?

By how much must purchases be increased to receive x per cent higher discount? Would this be worth the extra storage cost?

How well regarded is the firm by suppliers? Do we think they take advantage of us?

What alternative sources of supply are there?

Have we investigated own-branding?

What is the cost of backward integration, i.e. what is the cost of buying into our sources of supply?

What margins do our competitors receive?

What retail prices do they charge?

Is our charging system efficient?

Is it being carried out in a systematic manner?

Is the delivery system appropriate?

How much does it cost? Is it cost effective?

How controlled are mark downs?

WAGES

If payroll is computerised, how does it match up on a cost/efficiency basis with manual procedures?

If wage expenses are initially computed at branch level what controls are there?

What are the loopholes?

Is it worth setting up an audit team?

How can wage costs be reduced? By work study, setting establishment standards, more close control of recruitment?

What is the average sale per assistant?

What is the average gross and net profit contribution per assistant?

What is the comparative wage percentage per branch when net cost of sales is excluded?

What *are* the establishments per branch?

What is the mix of full time and part time staff per branch? Are they appropriate?

RENT/RATES

Are the correct rent and rates being charged to each branch?

Are freeholds being charged an economic rent?

How do rent and rates compare with charges on flanking or similar properties?

Are sub-rents being charged into the unit account?

Has there been any attempt at securing a rate reduction due to traffic management schemes or other alterations in the pedestrian environment?

GENERAL EXPENSES

What is the basis of delivery charges? Are they fair to each branch?

Can more efficient (more cost effective) lighting be installed?

Are there any rules for use of heating in summer?

Are telephone calls logged?

Have staff been educated in the use of the telephone?

Are cold counters kept at optimum temperatures?

Is it cheaper for cleaning to be done by a national contractor rather than by a local firm?

Do certain fixtures and decorations deteriorate quickly?

What is the usage of paper bags and wrapping paper?

SHRINKAGE

Do staff take food products off sale at break time as unauthorised 'perks'?

Are goods checked in immediately after delivery by the manager or authorised assistant?

How adequate is the supervision at actual time of delivery?

Are staff searches made before they leave the premises?

What is the wastage rate on best selling daily lines?

Is the wastage allowance fair, appropriate, open to abuse or is it merely swallowed up in the unit accounts?

Are security organisations used for spot checks?

If so, what is their success rate? How does it compare with other security organisations, store detectives, supervisory checks?

How foolproof are the cash registers in use?

Is there a schedule of registers issued, and is it checked regularly? Are transfers, defective tills, replacements logged?

What checking procedures are there for changing £5 or higher denomination notes?

How are over deliveries or wrong deliveries processed?

Is the credit note system foolproof?

Can the soilage/breakage rate be identified and checked?

How thorough is the check on goods at receipt? Does it screen units or only outers?

How secure are suppliers' packs at delivery?

Does the manager check date stamps on perishable goods at delivery?

What checks are there on stocktaking?

INDEX